Copyright © 2021 Andrew Wilson

All rights reserved.

ISBN: 9798562539069

This book is dedicated to my son, Lucas Wilson, who was its catalyst.

Thank you to my parents and my teachers for the moral and ethical upbringing that has allowed me to navigate the world with relative ease throughout my life.

I also owe a debt of gratitude to all the friends who inspired, supported and offered me their feedback in the process of writing this book. Thank you to Helder, John, Lynn, Craig, Alan, Ana, Diana and Milena for your contributions and words of support.

Finally, and very importantly, a big thank you to my editor Barbara Wilson from www.pensatostudios.com without whom this book would not be as pleasurable to read. (barbara@pensatostudios.com)

"[T]hou shalt love the Lord thy God with all thy heart, and with all thy soul, and with all thy mind, and with all thy strength: this *is* the first commandment. And the second *is* like, *namely* this, Thou shalt love thy neighbour as thyself. There is none other commandment greater than these."

Mark 12:31

Contents

Introduction
1 Shokunin kishitsu in men
2 Training wheels
3 Defining characteristics
4 Man and modern man
5. Tolerance
6 Fear
7 Having an opinion
8 Being a role model
9 Moments of truth
10 Discipline
11 Courage
12 Learning to take a knock
13 Respect
14 Care and compassion
15 Choosing your friends wisely
16 Programming
17 Authenticity
18 Integrity
19 Trust
20 Loyalty
21 Responsibility and accountability
22 Selfishness
23 Change
24 Acceptance
25 Fairness
26 Self-control
27 Moderation

28 Consistency
29 The internet of things
30 The media
31 Government
32 Timing
33 Forgiveness
   Old chapters
       Wokeness or wokery
       Sexuality
       Race

How to be a good hu(man)

Introduction

This book is dedicated to the concept of
職人気質
Shokunin kishitsu
In men

One day many years ago, I was in my kitchen talking to a 16-year-old boy, my son, about some aspect of life. I was "off on one" as I usually am, waxing lyrical about different points of view on some subject I am now at a complete loss to remember. The only thing I do remember is that, once I had stopped to pause for breath, my son turned to me and said, "You should write this stuff down. People would be interested." I remember thinking at the time that he seemed to mean it genuinely and wasn't just trying to make his old man feel good, and I held on to that thought – for years and years.

      Six years on, and I am now revisiting that conversation. A lot has happened in those six years, and I have had an opportunity to revisit much of my life in the intervening time. Many people around me have been sending similar messages to me, like the one my son sent my way back in 2014, and so I find myself in the position once again of trying to write a book. I have written one before on an incredibly boring yet vital topic of productivity. I have been trying to update it for the last six years and have failed miserably. I'm afraid, no matter how vital the book may seem to be, I can't seem to find the creative "whatsit" required to generate enough effort to finish it. Instead, recent events in my life have made me realise the possible value of some of the other things I know, and the massively beneficial nature that knowledge may have on a certain population of people in this world.

I am of course talking about men – young men to be precise. Young men these days are growing up in a world that is increasingly complex and difficult to deal with. Men make up the highest proportion of suicide in the developed world[1] and that is such a sad statistic it makes me want to try to do something about it.

I believe that much of the reason for this appalling statistic is that we (men) have forgotten how to be men and we have allowed the rights and opinions of others to overtake our own needs. I know that sentence alone will create an issue bigger than anything else I could say in today's online politically correct climate, but to all those who are picking up their pens and laptops to earnestly write and complain, I say to you – don't, your attitudes are part of the reason this book is writing itself into existence; take a moment, breath, read on, you may end up sympathising with the tenor of this book and take another look at where you sit with your own arguments.

I was lucky during my childhood. I grew up in over eleven different countries, with a strong father role model and a strong mother amongst a multitude of

---

[1] Suicide kills 1.4% of the global population each year – this is on a par with COVID 19! Young men between 15–25 are three times more likely to commit suicide than females, and 75% of the suicides occur in the poorer socioeconomic strata of society. (Source: WHO and the Samaritans.)

cultures with many different attitudes to society and the roles of men and women in those societies, so I come from a very broad church. I never had any problems defining my sexuality or my role in society; my morals, ethics and values were pulled from a mixture of family, school, religion, books and experience. I am what most people used to call a well-rounded and robust character. I "call a spade a spade" to coin a Yorkshire term and tend not to indulge in BS[2] or gossip and small talk. I am there for all those around me who need me. I take responsibility for all my actions, and I hold people to account for theirs. I have always thought that this was a normal way to be, but it seems as though it is not normal at all – and in fact I am regarded by many of a younger generation, and some older, as quite a scary proposition. This should not be the case. The fact that it is tells me that something has gone terribly wrong in the education of our young men, and we need to find a road back to a time when men were men and they knew what their role and place was in the world.

    I can tell you now that much of what I am going to say will seem totally inappropriate to some of you, and that is because I come from a different era and a different place in this world. I have not been indoctrinated by the news or magazines or chat shows or reality TV that infests our modern world – I don't even own a TV or a radio and haven't watched TV or the news for over twenty-four years. I realised as a 26-year-old that TV and news just made me angry and upset due to the lies and BS spouted on it, so I

---

[2] Bullshit

switched it off and have been a much happier man ever since.

You have to realise that writing a book is an incredible opportunity to write what *you* want to write, free of encumbrances and constraints. It should be a joy, to let your consciousness soar and let the words tumble on to the page. Be in no doubt, my intention here is to help. I want to help you get a few things straight in your heads so that you grow up to be a proper man who thinks and behaves correctly and fulfils his purpose in this complex world we live in. Your role cannot be overstated. Without strong role models, society starts to suffer. That is not to say that strong female role models are not needed too, but I know very little about women as I didn't bring up a daughter and I went to an all-boys school, so I missed a valuable part of my education in that regard. (Don't bother writing – you know who you are!) I tell you this by way of an explanation of why I am writing a book for men, by a man. All the women who have known me in my adult life will I hope attest to the fairness and respect with which I have and continue to hold them in. This is not a sexist rant at the fairer sex; this, gentlemen, is about being the best man you can be – and by that virtue offering to your womenfolk a strong, dependable, honest, hardworking partner.

1

職人気質

Shokunin kishitsu in men

The Japanese have a word for someone who dedicates themselves to the perfection of a craft: a Shokunin. Traditionally this referred to the lifetime dedication of a Japanese person to a particular job or craft. It offered the respect of all around them to the single-minded pursuit of perfection during their lifetime. I wondered when writing this book whether it would be possible to apply this ancient Japanese principle to the lifelong process of becoming a good man.

In Britain we used to have a phrase: a Gentleman. In Spain it is a Caballero. In fact, all societies have a version of the same thing – an ideal, which is defined by many characteristics of what a man should be and how he should behave and think about things.

In a sense Shokunin is about focussing on becoming the best you can be at something. It is a life-long commitment and focus towards whatever you set your mind to. The reason this is in a book on becoming a man is two-fold. Firstly, I see no reason why you cannot become your own Shokunin and use the principles of the idea to work towards becoming a shining example of a man who demonstrates all the best aspects of manhood in today's world. Secondly, I think that if you like the idea of Shokunin there is nothing wrong with taking that attitude into the work you decide to do in your life because as surely as you embark on that journey, the journey of your own self-development will also follow. You cannot be one without the other. To be a respected Shokunin, you must also be a respected man. The two depend equally on each other; they are almost inseparable.

You will see elements of Bushido, Buddhism, Stoicism and many other thought systems from around the world in this book; they are all worthy of your consideration and I hope very much that, if you find this book useful, you will embark on your journey as a Shokunin and learn more about these wonderful belief systems that exist and help so many other people in this world. My hope is that as your wisdom and knowledge increases you will adopt and integrate many of these lessons into your life as you take each step forward in your development as a man.

It has taken me many years, and many mistakes, problems, challenges and heartache to build a bridge across a very big river called life. I don't know whether I am all the way over the river yet; I suspect not, but looking back to the start of the bridge, it seems a very long way away now. I can't see the shoreline in either direction. I just know that the bridge I have built is sturdy and, if people want to follow, it can take the weight of many more people. So take a step forward with this book, and join me on my journey to becoming a good man.

2

Training wheels

Anyone who has learned to ride a bicycle will know what training wheels are: they are the side stabilising wheels that stop the bike falling over whilst you learn to ride a bike.

Well this is an important image to bear in mind when you read this book. For some of these topics, you can be riding with training wheels for many years. This isn't because you couldn't learn it any faster; it is because sometimes life doesn't present you with enough opportunities to learn and practise some of the things we are talking about. For some people mastering their courage is a daily event; for others it only happens a few times in their life. So don't be in a rush with this book. The lessons I am trying to impart to you are things you will be working on all the way to your deathbed.

I know this is an odd concept in today's society, where everything is measured online in "The three things you need to do to be successful", "The three things for a successful relationship", "Master your destiny in these easy steps". Well, my advice to you is ignore all of that – it's all bullshit. Life just does not work like that. Life is a continually changing landscape that you have to navigate every day for the whole of your life. The more you learn, the more you will realise just how little you know, and with that growing knowledge and the practice of the principles from this book, you will grow as a man and become wiser, and the world will become more complex with many shades of grey. This is why training wheels can be with us for a long time – because life just isn't an easy bike to ride.

So take small steps with this book, and come back to it as and when you need to, for the rest of your life if needs be. Don't try to rush anything. Life itself will dictate how quickly you learn the lessons that are given to you. All you have to do is to continue to try to ride the bike as well as you can and eventually you might not need training wheels.

Remember that small steps taken regularly carries a man a long way over the time of his life.

Here is one of my favourite little verses which I think sums up our journey through life. It is called "Autobiography in Five Short Chapters", by Portia Nelson.

> I walk down the street
> There is a deep hole in the sidewalk
> I fall in
> I am lost
> I am helpless
> It isn't my fault
> It takes forever to find a way out
>
> I walk down the same street
> There is a deep hole in the sidewalk
> I pretend I don't see it
> I fall in again
> I can't believe I am in the same place
> But it isn't my fault
> It still takes a long time to get out

I walk down the same street
There is a deep hole in the sidewalk
I see it is there
I still fall in
It is a habit
My eyes are open
I know where I am
It is my fault
I get out immediately

I walk down the same street
There is a deep hole in the sidewalk
I walk around it

I walk down another street

3

Defining characteristics

You are probably wondering where this book is going after the first few chapters. Well, let me start by giving you the broad brushstrokes of what a real man looks like. This is a bit tongue-in-cheek, but at its heart it really is about describing some of the physical and attitudinal differences between men and women.

1. A real man likes women. (We need them, mainly to counter our masculinity and macho tendencies. They bring balance to the universe and they give us purpose.)
2. A real man is generally hairier than a woman.
3. A real man is generally stronger and bigger than a woman.
4. A real man is generally more aggressive than a woman.
5. A real man generally is a danger to his own health.
6. A real man is a born hunter.
7. A real man does not give birth.
8. A real man likes to protect his loved ones.
9. A real man is capable of sensitivity and reflection, but doesn't feel the need to wear makeup.

10. A real man will accept when he has made a mistake and takes it on the chin without complaining.
11. A real man feels responsible for the welfare of his family.
12. A real man is kind and considerate of others.
13. A real man is polite and firm if necessary.
14. A real man does not lose his temper.
15. A real man never hits a woman or bullies others.
16. A real man is neither a racist, a sexist nor a homophobe, and is inherently tolerant.
17. A real man will lay down his life for his family.
18. A real man will work day and night to bring up his family and carry his burden quietly.
19. A real man likes the company of other men.
20. A real man has mates, and he does not let his mates down.
21. A real man honours his word, and his word is his bond.
22. A real man seeks to improve himself throughout his life, endeavouring to be a strong role model for all around him.
23. A real man brings up his children to not have the same failings that he has.
24. A real man will take his responsibilities seriously and take accountability for his actions at all times.
25. A real man will defend another unable to defend himself for no reason other than it is the right thing to do.

26. A real man is someone we all look to for inspiration and as an example of how to live a good life.
27. A real man does the "right thing" even when it is not in his best interests to do so.

There are probably a few more stereotypes you can think of as well. The important thing to bear in mind is that stereotypes are always based on reality. You sometimes hear people say "oh, that's just a stereotype" as if you have somehow over-simplified things. Well, stereotypes are an over-simplification, and that is the strength of them; they give us a very good guide of what we can assume is the "norm". That doesn't mean you have to *be* a stereotype, but it does mean that, if you stray too far away from the norm, people will start to talk and point fingers. So, as you can see, there is a lot to work on in just that short list. I hope this gives you a feeling of pride when you see this list and that much of it resonates with you already. As we go through this book, I will build on these elements and show you how to do them well and explain what is expected of you as a real man.

4

Man and modern man

Man has a pretty well-identified role on this planet, and there is at its heart biology. We are by nature larger, stronger, faster and more aggressive than our fairer sex. This is important. You will see messages all around you these days trying to persuade you that this is not the way of modern man: modern man can wear makeup, can be ambiguous about his sexuality and should cry more. (Over simplistic, I know, but you get the gist of it.) The list is endless – and I am sure you can add all sorts of things that you are being told to do – but the reality is that man is a simple soul and is actually only happy when his life is simple.

Let me describe some examples to you and see whether you agree.

All men need a cave – this is a stereotype, but you will find most stereotypes are born in reality. All men need a place to escape to, a room or a shed or a pub or somewhere where they can be left alone either with their own things, thoughts or the company of like-minded people. This is vital for men, the same way that they like to have "their chair" in the house, and "their place" at the table. The same way they like the keys to the car to remain in the "same place" so they are easy to find. Men like routines, they like people to be predictable, they like the kids to go to bed at the same time each day so they get their quiet hour in the evening. We like our time in the morning to read the paper and plan our day. You can see from this rapidly developing list that what we like most in life is things to go according to plan, to be able to find the screwdriver in the place where it should be, to have dinner at the same time, to be able to watch our favourite shows on TV in peace, to have a pint in the pub with friends on a Friday evening, to be able to retire to the cave for a bit of peace and quiet. We are simple creatures of habit.

That doesn't seem very inspiring, does it, but let's look at this another way. We want this in our lives because we will suffer untold stress and hardship working from the time we are sixteen to our seventies in order to put food on the table. We will work whether we are ill or well. We will sacrifice our lives to protect our family from whatever dangers there are, and we do all of this because we are men. It is our *role* in life. It is what our mothers, children and wives depend on in order to bring new life into this world. It is a contract; it is what we were born to do. As a result, when you look at a life of service like this, you can start to understand why we want life to be as simple as possible and as predictable as can be. Those elements of life I mentioned above are the life-raft that allows a man to remain centred, to remain constant. They are his oasis in a world that demands its pound of flesh for his entire life.

Now you can start to see hopefully, that there is a huge difference between the messages we are receiving as men these days from the media and certain very small minority groups about the reality of what we are on earth to do. I am not saying you can't wear makeup and be bisexual or even transexual if that is your bent, and you can choose not to marry and have children; you are perfectly entitled to do that.

In a sense this book is for all men no matter what you decide to define yourself as, but just be mindful that if you decide to stray too far from the "norm" some elements of this book may conflict with values you have chosen to adopt. If you feel that you don't relate to the book because you have chosen another path with your life, then that is fine also, just don't think you have any right to change everyone around you because of your personal choice. In the world I live in, and the majority of the world live in, I know what the role of a man is, and what his expectations should be.

The role of a man in the world is not an easy one, so, rather than trying to become more feminine or more "they", as the modern world want us to be, I urge you to be more masculine, to be more defined as a man and to live your life knowing what your contribution is and what you are due. Don't get confused by the small minority groups that are campaigning and creating so much noise and confusion. If you are a man, you are a man. It is really that simple and we have millions of years of history and practice at being a man, so there is nothing more really to be said on the matter.

5

Tolerance

This chapter started out completely different. It has been written and rewritten a dozen times at least. In the end, I realised that the reason I was getting myself in a muddle was because I had been affected by the desire to be overly sensitive to all the subjects I am going to cover in it. I was to all intents and purposes acting *woke*. I have now appreciated "wokery" for what it is – at its inception probably a genuine desire to help and now a form of tyranny of normal men. What started off in the 1940s as a simple call "to be aware" has morphed into something altogether different today. It is insidious in the way it inveigles its way into your consciousness and is almost parasitic in the paralysis it evokes when you try to comment on anything it has decided to lay claim to. As I write this, I am aware that I am still not saying what I want to say, and this is down to the confusion this subject has managed to create in modern society.

Wokery has developed into a modern linguistic cancer and, as such, should probably be subjected to the same level of treatment with which any other undesirable growth is dealt. I am sorry for whoever had the original and no doubt good intentions (a black United Mine Workers official in the USA, by all accounts) when he went about trying to increase the level of awareness of injustice in society through word play, but unfortunately it has been highjacked by an almost fascist fervour amongst its acolytes. The "wokerati" have done such a good job of weaponising the term in society that they are now subject to a full-scale push back by those who are not woke. The best we can say is that wokeness has increased awareness in the non-woke people about wokery. (See how easy it is to just start talking drivel when you talk about this subject!) To what end this helps anyone, I am at a loss to say.

You might be wondering why I am talking about this subject at all. Surely, if I am tolerant, I shouldn't hold these views? Well, I'm all for awareness, but when you introduce the idea that someone can be gender neutral and we should adopt a word like "zee" into the English language, I have to say enough is enough. To my mind, if you are calling yourself gender neutral, you are a hermaphrodite; that is the correct term, even though you don't fulfil even the basic criteria for hermaphroditism. What I actually see is confusion, both on the part of the people who feel that they can no longer identify with traditional society as well as with all of us around them. This book is inclusive – it is written for all men, no matter who they identify as – and I hope that the advice I give forms a metaphorical line in the sand. It is after all about common sense.

If you hear the phrase "you can't say that" or "you shouldn't say that" or "I can't believe you used that word", then you are probably in the company of a woke person. At this point it is important that you ignore what they have said and continue in a respectful and kind manner, as you should have been doing in the first place. We do not deliberately set out to harm others through what we say, unless we are being particularly unkind, so there should be no reason at all for someone to tell us what we can and cannot say. We have a right to talk as we wish to talk,. It is not for others to police our language; that, I am afraid, is almost the definition of fascism. So if you are a woke person then you must learn tolerance for the sake of others and for the sake of yourself. You need to realise that you are an immeasurably small number of people in the wider context of the globe and that, in fact, you have virtually no right at all to tell other people what they can or cannot say or do. You can chose to communicate in any fashion you wish to, but do bear in mind that many people simply will not have the foggiest idea what you are talking about as you have, to all intents and purposes, created another language. In fact, some of the conversations I have heard could have been from another planet.

    If you are struggling as a young person with the arena of wokery, please don't, unless you feel an absolute need to. It isn't necessary. Rather, concentrate on the lessons in this book and become a good man. If you master each of the chapters in this book, you will come to see how unnecessary wokery is. But likewise be tolerant of our woke friends. To them, the semantics of language are hugely important issues, and just as it is impolite for them to seek to correct us on how we talk, so it is impolite for us to comment on theirs. Just nod politely, smile, and move on.

Wokery has slipped in to the LGBTQ+ community as well – although many of my gay friends are at a loss to explain what it means or how it affect them. I rather think that just calling your gay friends by their name will be perfectly satisfactory; there is once again no need to learn a new language in order to communicate with them. But LGBTQ+ brings us on to another thing, again about tolerance, but also about the higher than usual rates of depression and suicide in this community.

It's difficult being gay in a society where you are only at most in 3.7 per cent of the general population, and as a minority you are always going to be sidelined by policy decisions and attitudes of mainstream society. Not only that, but gay people have a history of being persecuted – and still are in some countries. Being on the outside and subjected to intolerance is a terribly lonely thing, and that on its own contributes to feelings of depression. But why do we as a society subject gay people to this level of suffering? I think some of it hinges on a form of selfishness.

Let us start with love, we love our families deeply. It is with our families that we have the deepest emotional links. Part of that emotional link is an ancient and primordial desire for us as humans to reproduce. Part of the urge to reproduce is to create more copies of your own genetic code in the world – after all, that is what we are put on earth to do, biologically. Reproduction at its basic biological level is a selfish act between two people. It is a desire to produce, hopefully, better versions of yourself. You hope as parents that your children will also act in the same way because, that way, there will be yet more copies of you in the world. I know this idea seems a bit irrational, but bear with me. When your son or daughter discovers that they are gay, they are effectively threatening the future of your family's genetic pool. They are depriving their parents of the pleasure in their old age of seeing small versions of their children again and feeling secure in their last days on earth, knowing that they have done everything to secure the family line for the next hundred years or so. How disappointing.

"Disappointed" is probably the worst thing you can be with someone; it makes people feel wretched. The last thing on earth a child wants to do is disappoint a parent. We spend most of our lives trying to live up to our parents' expectations and please them if we can. Imagine what announcing your sexual orientation potentially means to your parents. Personally I can't, and it must be a very hard thing to do for anyone in that situation – and probably explains why so many gay men hide it from their parents. Parents also then heap indignity on top of this by becoming more selfish in their outlook as they then consider "what will our friends say?" In all of this, parents who behave in this way are acting through selfishness, weakness and cowardice. They should in fact read this book.

Being a gay man should not be a traumatic experience, and happily, through the bravery of many gay individuals, in many parts of the world the LGBTQ+ community now have rights and are recognised officially. But still intolerance persists and wokery by the trans movement is not helping at all.

So why does intolerance exist and what can we do about it? Again, it comes down to biology. As a species we treat difference with suspicion. Presumably in the mists of time, difference may have heralded danger, so we attacked it. We backed up this natural inclination by telling stories about the last time we, for example, saw a woman heal a sick person with herbs and how a few cows had died in neighbour's field the next day, and how the events must be connected, and she must be a witch. We feed on suspicion and rumour and imagination as a species, and it can be very harmful.

My position is this: I cannot for the life of me see why anyone would want to be unkind to another human being. That is my start point. So why would I be unkind to a young gay man? I am aware that I have the benefit of fifty years of life, and I have, for the most part, managed to implement most of this book in my life. But I want to take a shortcut here: **Be kind to people who are not like you. Be tolerant of their views and lifestyle choices.** I cannot be clearer than that.

Being kind and tolerant is not something we have been very good at as a society, and this is reflected in yet another area relating to race. Again, we are in a world of prejudice and intolerance. Frankly, I am dismayed that, in this day and age, we still have not learned to be fair and balanced in our dealing with our fellow man. Racism is everywhere, in all parts of the globe, and again it comes back to difference and our fear of it. We don't seem to be able to see past it to the soul of the person on the other side; we become transfixed by some physical aspect of someone. We are all humans, and we were all born by mothers who loved us and whom we adore back. We all had fathers and, for the most part, we all have our own children at some stage in our life. We all love a good party and enjoy holidays, good food, fun, laughter and love. We are all the same. The only difference between us is the rubbish we fill our heads with.

Again, this is a topic full of wokery. Indeed, it was Black rights in the USA that started wokery. But again it has been politicised and hijacked by a minority group and effectively weaponised. You now hear nonsense about "white privilege" and how if you are a white person you must be racist even if you don't yet know it. This again is complete nonsense and weaponised wokery at its worst. Yes, there is racism all over the world, and, no, it is not acceptable, but it is also not acceptable to accuse everyone that is not in your minority group of being unconsciously racist; that is simply absurd. So again the same advice prevails in this situation: if you find you are in a conversation about whether you are racist or not, or unaware of your privilege, etc., just smile, thank them for their time and move on. Believe me, I have been down this rabbit hole many times and the arguments used against you are a form of weaponised logic. The important thing to know here is that you can't win against the logic because it is flawed, so don't try. Non-engagement is the only defence you have.

So I am going to end this chapter by reiterating the importance of tolerance to you, as a young man, whether you are a young gay man, a young Black man or, for that matter, any man, any shape, size or colour. Tolerance is about pausing; it is about taking a moment to consider what your brain was telling you to do and then to rethink it. It is about seeing the fragile human in front of you who is really very much like you in the majority of ways. It is about pausing and asking yourself: Am I about to be kind and respectful? If the answer is no, you need to take note and go away and think why you have that attitude. The rest of this book will help you with that internal conversation.

Be kind, be respectful, be caring of others; it's simple really. You do not need to be woke or employ wokery; you do not need to be "anti" anything. You just need to treat your fellow man with care and respect. If you do this, you will be tolerant of others' views even when they choose not to be tolerant of yours. But this book is about making you a better man, so even when others do not extend to you the same courtesy you are extending to them, it shouldn't matter. You will continue to be polite, respectful and caring towards them. Only this way can we hope to stop the anguish that so many people feel in society.

6

Fear

As a young man, or indeed any man, in this world, you will find that for a lot of the time, to a greater or lesser extent, you will be fearful. This may be as simple as worrying about what someone might think of you, through to fearing that you might lose your job and not be able to pay the mortgage. Fear is with us one way or the other throughout our lives, and it can be very detrimental to your health and well-being if not understood and dealt with correctly.

Why do we have fear, you might ask? Well, to put it simply, we have fear as part of our inbuilt survival mechanism. Generally, it is quite useful to suddenly feel fear when faced by a charging lion, for example; it's your body's way of telling you that you need to do something fast to stop yourself getting eaten. In the good old days of prehistoric man this was a useful survival mechanism as it only happened occasionally and kept you alive. Nowadays we are bombarded with things that can make us fearful. Here are just a few as examples:

- Fear of what someone might think of you
- Fear of failure
- Fear of not being good enough
- Fear of losing your job
- Fear of not having enough money

- Fear of being told off
- Fear of not being loved
- Fear of dying
- Fear of others dying

Truly, the list is endless and in some part has to do with the complex society we have created and all the rules and expectations that have been setup around living in the modern world. Prehistorically all you needed to worry about was where to crap, what to hunt and eat, and where to sleep, preferably with a warm woman if available. Life was simple back then – if not a little more dangerous. But you get my point.

You will see in a number of these chapters that overcoming fear is at the heart of being a good man, a respected man, a man that can be trusted. So understanding fear and overcoming it are really important things for you to work on, probably for most of the rest of your life.

So here it is, the simple part, not the easiest part, just the simple part: to overcome your fear, you need to understand that it is based on what you think *might* happen in the future if you do or do not do something. You can choose to be paralysed by fear and allow the world to swallow you up or you can choose to *do* something.

Action overcomes fear. Once you are doing something to mitigate the fear you have, you will notice that the world starts to change around you, and what you thought was fearful becomes less fearful. If you are committed and continue to fight through the actions and make things happen then you create a solution where you no longer need to be fearful. An action can be a decision – you can decide that you will face whatever you are going to face no matter the consequences. Once you have made that decision, facing up to whatever it is you are facing is easier and less fearful.

The point here is that the future is different if you stand still, compared to the future if you step forward and start to shape it. One action (staying frozen) keeps you in one reality; the other action (shaping your future) takes you away from this reality and into another one.

What you find when you step out of one reality and into another one is that things mysteriously start to work for you and the situation gets better – to such an extent that you will often hear the common expression "I can't believe I didn't do this before!" Whenever you hear this expression, you know someone has just stepped-up, mastered something that they were fearful of, and *done* something to change their reality.

Fear is also infectious – it's catching. When you are in a group and you suddenly feel fearful and you don't know why, ask the person next to you. They will probably tell you that they also don't know why but they share your fear. Well, go and find out and put a plan of action together because just as fear is catching so is strength and courage.

This, my friends, is such an important lesson, and you will see in the coming chapters that you cannot do much of the work without learning to cope with and master your fears. You will, however find that doing some of the things that the following chapters suggest will help you to reduce the fears you have.

If you want to be a man, you need to master your fears first; after that, you will be able to help others master theirs too.

7

Having an opinion

With the amount of social media and the freedom to express ourselves, we would be forgiven for thinking that we are some of the most opinionated people on earth these days. But I am not sure that is true. I rather think that we echo the thoughts of others and are too easily influenced by those who decide their opinions are more important than those of other people.

So let's start at the beginning – what is an opinion? An opinion is what you believe in. It is based on all the relevant information you have gathered through reading and talking to people and through the thinking you have done on the subject. This all leads you to have an opinion. An opinion doesn't have to be "right" or politically correct, or "on-message". An opinion is yours and yours alone and you are perfectly entitled to hold it and share it with others when you think it is appropriate.

Everyone has an opinion and has the same rights as you do to hold their opinion on things. So it should be clear that we should respect each other's rights to hold an opinion. However, these days, with social media, its almost like a witch hunt where people seek to attack others with different opinions to their own, or to opinions regarded as the dominant view. This is disrespectful to everyone.

When you hold an opinion, it is important that, whenever you come across a really persuasive argument against your point of view, you should take that away with you and reconsider your point of view and maybe modify your opinion slightly. There is nothing wrong with doing this. In fact, holding on to an opinion long after it has been shown to be ridiculous is stubborn and silly. So don't be afraid to change your opinion if you feel you need to. By the same token, if you think that the counter arguments to your opinion are totally stupid, you are quite entitled to say so and hold on to your opinion, but you must say why you disagree with the counter argument – you can't just say "because". Another important point is that you don't have to get bogged down in ever-more-complex counter-arguments. If a counter-argument doesn't immediately challenge your point of view and you don't immediately understand it – it may be that it is probably not worthy of consideration at this moment in time. I say this because we often don't actually know why we hold an opinion, and we therefore get confused when trying to explain it to others. If you can't give your opinion clearly and concisely and persuasively, you might want to keep it to yourself until you understand it better.

So here is a piece of advice for when you are on social media and you want to say something and lots of people are trying to change your mind. Just simply state your opinion; you are entitled to it and it is valid. If other people get riled up and angry because of it, that is *their* problem not yours. You have simply laid out your view, as is your right to do. If others don't think you should hold that view, they are effectively engaging in a form of intellectual bullying by trying to get you to change your stance in their favour. If this is what they are doing, just make it clear that you have stated your point of view, and if they don't like it, in the words of Stephen Fry "so fucking what!"[3]

I have been known – am known even – to have some strange opinions about things. They are strange to people around me because those people have not lived my life, read the books I have read, and are probably not wired like I am, intellectually. But I am nonetheless sought after by people looking for an alternative view to the general narrative they are listening to. Why am I telling you this? I am telling you this to reassure you that there is nothing wrong with seeing the world in a different way and having opinions that others don't agree with; it is part of becoming the unique and authentic person you need to become. So think about where your opinions come from the next time you are offering them to someone, and ask yourself: "Is this my opinion or someone else's? Do I agree with it or not? Do I in fact have a slightly different view of this and should I share that instead?"

Welcome to becoming yourself.

---

[3] "It's now very common to hear people say, 'I'm rather offended by that.' As if that gives them certain rights. It's actually nothing more ... than a whine. 'I find that offensive.' It has no meaning; it has no purpose; it has no reason to be respected as a phrase. 'I am offended by that.' Well, so fucking what." Stephen Fry. I saw hate in a graveyard, *The Guardian*, 5 June 2005.

8

Being a role model

What do I mean by being a role model? A role model is basically someone you look to as a guide on how to think and behave – a hero if you like, someone you admire. They will usually be someone who has a set of characteristics that you find admirable and with which you identify and want to emulate. A role model usually inspires in you a desire to copy that person and to try to become some aspect of that person.

We find characteristics in certain people admirable – for example, the characteristic of generosity. Perhaps we see a footballer we admire on television talking about a children's charity he supports, and we decide that giving to charity is a good thing. So the next time we have a bit of money, we also give to charity, and as a result we feel good about ourselves and feel as if we are a bit like our football hero. We feel similar and we feel proud of what we have done. We have in fact emulated the behaviour of a role model and in some part become a little bit like him.

It might be that by having decided to give to a charity, a friend of yours sees you do this and starts to admire that characteristic in you and decides that in a small way you are a role model to them and they too decide to give to charity.

You see, by demonstrating admirable behaviours and beliefs, you start to influence the people around you and slowly those admirable characteristics start to spread through society, and we start to become a better society as a result of that.

As you grow older you will come to realise that what you do, and how you do it, rubs off on all sorts of people around you – from your children to your work colleagues and the trainees that come through work. They in turn take the good bits of you and pass this on to their children and work colleagues, families and friends. So by the time you are eighty, there are potentially sixty to seventy years' worth of people who you have influenced with a little bit of you in the world, and they are busy spreading your influence further afield long after you are gone.

Take some of the most famous people in the world – Gandhi, Churchill, Nelson Mandela, Martin Luther King Jr, Abraham Lincoln to just name a few. Along with many others, these great men represented some of the best characteristics of role modelling in our history, and that is why they are remembered and talked about to this day and held up as examples of how to behave.

Now don't get me wrong, a lot of role models have catastrophic faults as well, and that is normal; we are all flawed human beings. What is important is that at critical moments in their lives when it was vitally important that they did the right thing, they did, and as a result the world is a better place for it. That is what they are remembered for and why we can forgive some of their failures. For these men, when the crunch came and they were called upon, they had to stand tall and take the ultimate responsibility for their actions and the effects it would have on millions around them. They took on that responsibility, stood firm and took the decisions they knew they had to take because it was the right thing to do. They didn't make decisions because it was the easy road to take, or the ones most beneficial to them, they stepped into the unknown and risked everything because it was the right thing to do. As a result of that courage and responsibility they are exulted for the rest of their lives and in history books ever after and looked upon as shining examples of what we should be like.

Every one of us faces these smaller events throughout our lives, whether it is a decision to stand up for someone who is getting bullied even when you are not involved and don't have to be involved, through to standing by your family to ensure your children have a father despite your marriage being on the rocks. It applies to telling the truth to your boss when you don't like the way they are managing you, through to leaving a job because the company is doing something you don't agree with. These are all decision points, points of principle, defining points in your life that allow you to grow and lead and show the way we should behave versus the way we are behaving. These are points where we signal to those around us what the correct actions is, and by doing so become a role model to some of those around you. You lead from the front, as a strong, independently minded man, someone who your children will want to follow, emulate and talk about with their friends, someone your children will be proud to call their father.

9

Moments of truth

In the previous chapter, when I talked about being a role model, I talked a bit about "moments of truth".[4] What do I mean about these moments, what are they and how do we know we have arrived at one of these defining moments?

Well, simply put, a moment of truth is a situation where you are faced with an impossible decision. It normally means you are going to have to make a decision that will have some negative impact on yourself if you do it. There is normally an alternative that is either beneficial to you or at least looks as if it may get you off the hook. When you look at it closely you can see that taking the easy route is only easy for you and normally results in someone else or many other people suffering as a result, and may not completely remove you from the consequences. The correct path, the hard path, the path that hurts you normally means that others are not negatively affected or are affected to a lesser degree. This is a terrible decision to make; after all, who makes a decision to harm themselves rather than trying to take the easy path. Most people's initial desire is to make life easy for themselves, and to avoid the effort and pain of

---

[4] The development of this idea and the borrowing of the expression comes from a book I read many years ago called *Moments of truth*, Jan Carlzon, 1989. The expression has always resonated with me.

doing something. A real man knows what he has to do, and he steps forward and does what is right for everyone around him and lives with the consequences of that action. In some ways it takes a little act of bravery to make a decision like this and a commitment to *do* something.

You see, once you make the correct decision, you are free from guilt. You can hold your head up high and feel virtuous about yourself. You can live with yourself knowing you did the right thing by others. You were a man, you made the right decision, you lived your life as you would expect others to do, you were an example to others, and you have the unspoken gratitude of those around you. You have elevated yourself above those lesser men around you who chose to cut and run. You have become an example to others, and how you bare your burden and suffering as a result says more about you than anything most people can ever do in their lives. You grow, you become magnificent and you radiate to all around you.

That is what a moment of truth is, and what it represents to us as men. It is our purpose in life. It is what we were put on earth to do. It is for our children and our children's children. Do not for a minute underestimate the power of these moments and the effect they have on you, those close to you, around you, and the wider audience that get to hear about your decision. The very foundation of society and its success ultimately depends on you being strong enough to make the "right" decision come hell or high water at these critical "moments of truth". They are what define you, what make you special, what make lesser men want to grow and be better men, what elevates us as a sex in this modern world.

So the next time you are at a moment of truth, take a deep breath, grow a pair and make the right decision and live with it. "Suck it up" as they say in modern parlance, be the man you always wanted to be. It's your moment; it belongs to you and no one else. It will be one of many stepping stones on your road to becoming the example of manhood this world needs and so desperately wants.

10

Discipline

Okay, on to the hard bit! Discipline. You cannot be effective in life without it – it really is that simple. You will have seen YouTube videos by marines and special forces, by gurus, by Ted talkers, you name it, they are all talking about it. The fact that everyone is harking on about it so much should tell you something: we are generally not very good at it!

Why are we not good at it? Well, for a start it's hard to do. Given the choice between having a couple of beers with mates down the pub and sitting for two hours working on the next project you have to do, or reading that next book that will get you a promotion, nine out of ten of us will go to the pub with our mates. It's that simple – we would rather have fun than work hard, and if we have to work hard we definitely want to have fun afterwards!

But discipline is a curious thing. If you start small and gradually build up your discipline, it is not hard work at all, but so many gurus will have you believe you need to transform yourself. I don't believe that; I think discipline is multifaceted. Start with getting up at a certain time in the morning. It doesn't need to be at 5 am like the productivity gurus tell you, but it needs to be at a time that gives you enough time to do your stuff in the bathroom, have breakfast and feel ready to leave the house. By the same token, if that time is 7 am and you can only get up easily every day without feeling tired after you have had eight hours of good sleep, then by definition you need to be asleep by 11 pm the night before. So you have a basic set of disciplines defined for you already here. If you stick to these disciplines, then you will automatically start to see that you apply disciplines around other areas of your life. For example, if you need to be asleep by 11 pm, you will leave the pub, or stop work, or whatever you are doing, by 10 pm in order to be able to complete all the things you need to do before you go to sleep.

You can see where I am going with this, and I am sure as a young man you are thinking, as Lord Black Adder would say, "What fresh lunacy is this?" Well, all I can say is that if you don't want to introduce discipline into your life just yet, then don't. You will eventually come to realise – as you watch those around you who are more disciplined pull ahead in their careers and lives – that perhaps discipline is a good thing after all. You need to start early and put the foundations in because it takes years to become disciplined.

Just to give you an example: for years, I tried to be disciplined with myself, but clients would ring and ask if I could be somewhere for a meeting at 7 am on a Monday morning and I would always say "yes". I always said "yes" because I didn't want to upset my client and I didn't want them to think I was lazy. So I would get up at 3 am and drive all the way to where the meeting was. I would have the meeting and then spend the rest of the day unable to stay awake or think straight. (Thirty years of doing this cost me my health by the way.) Eventually, after my job had nearly killed me, I had no choice but to say "no" to requests like this and to book a time that I could make. It was a complete revelation to me to find out that, most of the time, my clients had never considered the consequence of their request. (This probably explained why they had never said "thank you" for attending those early meetings in the previous thirty years!) These days all my clients are more than happy to rearrange a meeting time that is suitable or convenient if asked to do so for good reason. The only reason I ask now is because my health has made me more disciplined about how I run my day. As a result I am fresher, more awake and more productive than I have ever been – good for me and my clients. This is called a win–win, but sometimes you don't even know it's available to you unless you ask. A very wise man once told me "if you don't ask, you don't get". I thought I understood the message fully, but it took me thirty years to realise how widely that piece of advice could be applied.

    The reason I am telling you this story is because I can imagine you might be thinking *my god, my boss would kill me if I said no*. Well, that is where the discipline comes in and the hard work begins. It is about setting standards for yourself and interacting with the world around those standards, no matter how hard it may seem. Ultimately, what your boss thinks is irrelevant if it leads to you keeling over with a heart attack or a mental breakdown from allowing yourself to be driven so hard.

Do you see now what I mean about discipline? It is not just about activities that you do every day, or rules that you put in place. It is having the mental discipline to run your life according to these rules and to adhere to them when others try to make you do something different. Discipline requires huge mental strength and huge courage. And that is why we are so bad at it. That is precisely why it is so important to your success and happiness in life and why you must start to become disciplined with yourself and your life. It is also a reason why most of the motivational speakers you hear talking about it are ex-marines as they are hard men. What they don't tell you is that they all started just like us and it was the army that instilled the disciplines over many years until it became second nature for them. Luckily for most of us, we don't need to risk our lives to learn discipline; we just need to start to build on it a little each day and continue doing so for the rest of our lives.

11

Courage

We mentioned how hard discipline was and we hinted at the courage required sometimes to maintain discipline in the face of overwhelming odds – such as your boss ordering you to do something that will not fit with your plan for life. But courage is such an important subject that it was even described by the ancient Greeks as something of critical importance to people. They had a word for it – parrhesia, which means "a verbal activity in which a speaker expresses his personal relationship to truth, and risks his life because he recognises truth-telling as a duty to improve or help other people".[5] Most of us these days can't imagine a situation where we would risk our lives by speaking the truth, but we can imagine risking our jobs, or our reputations, for example.

    Courage, much of the time, is about mastering your fear of a situation and marshalling the inner strength to tackle something that is fearful. Sometimes when people talk of another's courage they say "he was utterly fearless". What they mean is having the courage to master your fears in order to step forward and do the right thing in the moment. In effect, having a moment of truth and deciding to take action.

---

[5] From Michel Foucault's speech, "The Meaning and the Evolution of the Word Parrhesia."

Being a moral man and someone that can be trusted and depended upon requires vast amounts of courage. There will be times when you have promised to do something for someone, or you can see that something bad will happen if you don't intervene. Think for example of someone being bullied, harassed or assaulted. You could just turn a blind eye and walk away, or you could do something. The feeling you get of butterflies in your stomach that makes you want to turn the other way is actually your body's way of telling you that you need to step up and help. Your conscience often tells you what the right thing to do is, and your body responds by making you a little scared. When you get that feeling you have a moment of truth arriving, an opportunity to act as a role model for all those around you who are just watching and not doing anything. You have an opportunity to display courage and lead. Nine times out of ten, when one man leads, others quickly follow, but it takes huge courage to be the first one to step forward and make a difference.

I will be honest, you don't always win by being courageous; sometimes you make yourself distinctly unpopular, sometimes you get hurt, and you can even become the target of the bullying or aggression you are trying to stop. But as I always say to people, you always feel good afterwards about doing whatever you had to do, and believe it or not the people around you respect you a great deal more for trying to do the right thing. Courage is its own reward, as some rightly say. I have to put a warning here: I am not advocating that you jump into the first fight you see as a way of demonstrating to yourself your new found courage.

Please pay some heed to your personal physical and mental safety as well. If you think you are likely to get badly hurt as a result of your new found courage, you might want to adopt the traditional mantra: "Discretion is the better part of valour."

In your working life, you will need courage – courage to make the leap to a new job, courage to invest money in a new venture or idea, courage to stand up to your boss, courage to walk away from situations you know are wrong. You have to have courage to be successful; success is founded on courage. Don't think for a minute that these hugely successful entrepreneurs didn't need courage. They still do. They still lie awake at night sweating when they have to make a big decision that could make or break them. Everyone needs courage.

So the next time you are faced with a situation where you would much rather just walk quietly away or ignore a situation, take a moment to consider what it means to be a real man and master your fear and generate the necessary courage to step up and make a difference. Trust me, no matter how terrifying it might seem, every time you master your fear and make a difference you take a step forward as a man, and each time it gets a little bit easier to be courageous.

Do it for yourself, do it for those around you, role model the behaviour, make a difference in people's lives around you; and to your own. Be brave, be strong and be a man.

12

Learning to take a knock

We used to learn this every day at school at games time, when the big boys won whatever game or sport we were participating in. It's no fun losing and it certainly isn't any fun losing all the time. That's why in the UK we started giving medals and prizes to people for participating; to make them feel good about just taking part. Unfortunately, this has led to an entire generation of people who think they should just get a prize for turning up.

Life isn't like that unfortunately. You can turn up, but if you don't plough the field, seed it and water it, you are not going to get anything out of it. Life is actually very unforgiving; it is quite hard in fact, and some would say *very* hard. That isn't good or bad; it just is what it is. Some people have horrible lives and some people have privileged lives, and there is a tendency for those who are having a horrible time to look at those privileged souls with envy and disdain. Well, let me tell you, appearances can be deceptive. We all struggle, but we all have different struggles with different stresses and strains. No one escapes, no one is immune, so stop looking over the fence and feeling hard done by.

The measure of a man is his ability to take a knock and get back up and carry on and learn the lesson he was dealt.[6] It's really that simple. Sitting around whinging and blaming others for your misfortune is just a waste of time. Instead, you should take the view that life is just a very long to-do list of things that range from tasks you hate doing, to tasks you love doing, and all of them have to be done. Getting knocked-back should be a regular occurrence in your life – if it is not, you are probably not trying very hard. You should expect it, and you should just shrug it off and get back to the list of things you have to do. Don't complain, just get up, brush yourself down, and ask yourself "what have I learned from that experience?" Then move on. Success is only achieved by moving forward, by learning hard lessons, by learning and doing things better the next time, by not giving up.

Some of you may say, "Yes, but what happens if it's a really big knock, like losing everything and ending up on the street without money or shelter" or something like that. Well, all I can say is that it is even more important that you get back up and crack-on. In that situation, sitting around feeling sorry for yourself is only going to make matters worse. I learned this from a Frenchman called Alan, who washed dishes in a restaurant I was working in. Alan was a hippie – or at least he had started out as one. I think he still was one at heart. He had developed a very healthy drug habit in the 1960s and was a committed alcoholic. In the end

---

[6] If you ever saw the film Rocky about a famous boxer in the USA you will know the almost universally quoted phrase: "But it ain't about how hard you hit. It's about how hard you can get hit and keep moving forward; how much you can take and keep moving forward. That's how winning is done!"

he was on the street and in a very bad way altogether. Somehow Alan found the inner resources to turn all of this around: he started taking jobs removing the rubbish from the back of restaurants for a few pennies, he managed to get his doctor to put him on medication to support his drug habit, and he started to wash dishes for people in restaurants for cash. Gradually, day by day over seven years, he clawed his way back to a point where he was a recovered alcoholic, with a small house and a full-time job washing dishes. He was grateful for his work, and he knew he had achieved something. He knew he had saved his life. He also taught other people his story as well by way of being inspirational.

    I loved Alan, he was a wonderful human being with a truly interesting story of how to fight for your place in life. Alan had taken more knocks than most of us ever have to deal with in a lifetime, and he had overcome them. What he taught me was that no matter how hopeless a situation looks, you have to continue to move forward, to fight to better your situation. Every gain is a small victory. You should never give up hope.

13

Respect

Respect is vital to your survival. You will find that you can respect anyone if you try hard enough, but you just need to look carefully and give them, and yourself, enough time.

Respect is one of those things we are very hasty to give out and take back. Sometimes, we give respect to people just because we are told to do so, and sometimes we don't give respect to people because, frankly, we think they are idiots undeserving of our respect.

Well, let's make this simple: **Respect everyone equally**. I mean it, everyone, equally. Respect them as human beings first, then as sons and daughters, mothers, fathers, cousins, grandfathers, grandmothers, respect them all for just being human and being part of the same planet that you live on.

We all manage to grow up and contribute in some way to life on this earth, and if you can't see how people are contributing or adding value, then you need to look a little harder and for a bit longer, because I guarantee you will find something worthy of your respect, no matter how small. Sometimes the respect comes when you least expect it, either through kindness and generosity in a time of need, or a caring word here or there. Small things that, when you consider everything else that the person is going through, can seem enormous at the time.

I once heard a story of a traveller in Africa. He was in a poor village with the kids all around him. The kids had no clothes, no schooling – nothing. In our world we wouldn't generally respect people like this. But the kids smiled and were friendly to the traveller, so he took out a chocolate bar and gave it to one of the kids. The child grinned, took the bar, split it in half and offered the man half of the bar, before splitting the other half amongst his friends.

Now you tell me what there isn't to respect in that story – a poor child with nothing, who offers friendship with a smile and shares badly needed food with the person giving it (who doesn't need it) before sharing the rest with his friends. That's what it means to be human. That's what it means to offer respect to fellow man. If you can do that one thing alone, you will be a far greater man than most around you.

You take this respect and you offer it to anyone you meet. You should meet people with genuine friendship and a smile, grant them your time and listen to them, take an interest in them, and help if you can. You shouldn't belittle them, get angry with them, or make them feel small. These are all aspects of giving respect to people. Here are more examples of things you can do to show respect:

- Treat the person with the care you would offer a good friend
- Be kind in the things you say to them

- Be supportive of things they say (remember, you might not agree with them, but you are respecting their views and their right to have them)
- Be polite
- Try to accommodate them in their needs if you can (clearly this is not a permanent solution, but something you might do as a one off – like choosing a Chinese restaurant if you know that is the food they like to eat)
- Be respectful towards their culture and background
- Be open and honest with them

Now, you may not always get respect back, but that is their problem not yours. The moment you think it's your problem you really have a problem. No, if they are not respectful in return, you can either point this out to them, or just ignore it. I always think it is better to demonstrate my respect for someone regardless of whether they reciprocate. In some ways, by doing this I keep the moral high ground and can feel good about myself when we part ways. You can't expect everyone in the world to be a gentleman – it just doesn't work that way – but that shouldn't stop us from maintaining standards. In the end, you simply will not keep in touch with anyone who doesn't respect you, so why get upset.

14

Care and compassion

This isn't just something you give your Gran. Being caring and being compassionate are part of being human; they are either the foundation of love or the result of love for another person.

Can you remember when you were a kid and you fell over and grazed your knee? You went running back to your mum or dad crying. Do you remember how good it felt when they took you into their big strong arms and held you, dried your tears, told you it would be alright and put a plaster on your knee? Remember how *good* that felt. Well, from time to time as adults we need that feeling too.

Just knowing and being able to give your mate a hug when a member of his family dies, or sitting quietly whilst a friend cries in front of you and offloads all the horrible things that have happened to him/her that day – these are examples of care and compassion. They are what make us truly superhuman people to others.

It's not just people who you know that care and compassion can be extended to. You can extend it to the starving children worldwide, to the mistreated animals we see everywhere, to the planet that is being destroyed. Caring deeply and having compassion can be a very powerful force for change, not just in you but also in others.

As a boss, you should care for your employees and should expect that from your boss too. Your family one day will need your care and compassion, your wife will need it, and your children will certainly need it. You are probably starting to see that a life without care and compassion is hard to achieve in reality, so you might as well embrace it. I say that because there is an awful lot of "messaging" in the world today about being driven, money focussed, uncaring, rational, neutral, etc. Well, I don't subscribe to that philosophy, and I don't think you should either.

I'll tell you why: the moment you hold your new born baby in your arms is the moment you truly know what care and compassion is. You can have had the most awful life up to that moment, suffered great hardships, and hate the world in so many ways for the misery heaped upon you. But your child in your arms is proof that the world has the potential to renew itself. It is a moment when, no matter how hard and heartless you are or have become, you are consumed by love for this new little life in your arms. This new soul is born to you and is completely dependent on your care and compassion for its survival and happiness.

For many the thought of care and compassion is a dream. So many of us suffer at the hands of others, and I can hear people saying "But how can I be caring and compassionate when I'm being abused by someone?" And my heart bleeds when I hear someone say this. In so many ways, care and compassion is taught, and without a suitable teacher we don't know how to do it properly. Many people hurt other people because that is what they were taught as they grew up. Others do it as a defence mechanism because they are afraid of the world. There are in fact hundreds of reasons why people hurt each other. But we are all capable of care and compassion to some degree, and it is up to us to practise this vital skill with all around us so that we live in a gentler, kinder and more supportive world.

There are some who say you sometimes need to be "hard to be kind"; this doesn't mean you have to be heartless. Being hard on someone for their own good as long as it comes from a place of care and compassion is forgivable. Sometimes people don't listen or are unable to hear what you are saying. Sometimes they hear what you are saying but cannot understand it or are unable, without a push, to do what is necessary. This is called "tough love". Being a caring person and a compassionate person will allow you to be tough when the situation arises without being accused of being heartless. Your track record needs to speak for itself. So you can see that being caring and compassionate is not always about being soft and cuddly. It is a hard skill to master, where you tread a fine line between being caring and being soppy and wet – you need to stop before people start to take advantage of your good nature.

If you can master this skill in your life, you will become a special kind of man to all those around you. You will also become the kind of man who will ask for help when you need it because you understand how valuable care and compassion is. No man is an island;

we are all deeply connected to those around us and the wider world, so show care and kindness to all that need it when it is called for.

15

Choosing your friends wisely

Ask yourself how many of your friends you have actually chosen. Then, ask yourself how many friends you have just accumulated as part of being in either a particular place or time. I think in general we tend to accumulate friends as a result of what we are doing at the time, but we rarely assess whether they are truly people we want to call friends or not.

Most of the people you know are not friends. They may be friendly, and they may be people you can associate with and go for a drink with, but they are not actually friends. We can only have a few friends in life – maybe as few or as many as six good friends; the rest are acquaintances. Friendship, and by this I mean genuine friendship, is a bond a bit like loyalty. It requires effort, although sometimes it feels effortless. But with friends come expectations about what you will be prepared to do for each other.

It is amazing how many people fall in with the "wrong crowd" thinking they have friends. This is partly down to many of us just feeling lonely on our own and wanting the company of others and partly down to poor judgement about who *we* are and what we want. So when you find a really good crowd of people or you are adopted by a crowd of people, you naturally start to view them as friends. This is the wrong way to go about things. Friends require a lot of attributes, some of which I have listed below:

- Friends are people you want to be around and spend time with.
- Friends will always give you their time if you need it.
- Friends will help in any way they can if you are in trouble.
- Friends are generally people you have kept in touch with or known for a long time.
- Friends are your first port of call for advice and discussion.
- Friends will suffer with you if it's necessary to help out.
- You would give all of the above to your friend (it's a two-way process, you see).

With the advent of social media we seem to believe that we have lots and lots of friends, but this is an illusion. There are no virtual friends in this world. Friendship is one of those things where you actually need to be physically present for most situations. So don't go looking for friends in the virtual sphere of life. These are not even acquaintances; they are simply avatars of people that may or may not exist.

Gangs are generally not a good place to go looking for friends either as their members are more likely to follow the group than an individual. And although sometimes gang members may act like a friend, there will be, more often than not, situations where they behave like the opposite of a good friend.

A good friend is a friend for life, generally. You value them as much as they value you, and as a result you are both prepared to make the necessary effort to invest in that friendship. You can tell a lot about a person from the friends he keeps, so always remember that friends are a reflection of you. They are in some ways a reflection of your values and your views in life. Sometimes when we look at our friends we might think *are these people really who I am*? If the answer is no, then you may have some work to do in finding friends that more closely reflect who you are.

Don't worry if this seems hard and you don't seem to have many friends; you actually collect your friends thought your life. So if you consider that you are going to have only a handful of truly good friends, that means you will probably start off with only one or two, and gradually over your lifetime you will get a few more. You may look around and see many people who appear to have lots of friends, but they are in fact "popular" and that is quite another thing. Popular people have lots of people around them, for whatever reason that may be, but very often they still have only a few good friends. So don't think that popularity is in any way an indicator of how many friends you have.

Friends make life better, more fun and less stressful. That is why you need to choose them well. If you have a bunch of good friends you are more likely to enjoy life. So don't be afraid to *choose* your friends and invest time in people you value. It's one of life's joys.

16

Programming

This is not the computer kind, although it has a lot of similarities. This is about the mental routines and the thinking patterns you have inside your head.

You probably believe that you are in complete control of your thoughts and how your mind works. I am sorry to tell you that nothing could be further from the truth. You are a collection of programs and systems of thinking that have been given to you from birth. You have about as much chance of having an original thought as a penguin does of finding fish in the Sahara desert.

Don't get depressed though, this is the good part. Once you know that you are programmed, you can start to dismantle that assigned programming and create your own.

So let's look at some of the obvious examples of programming:

- Your nationality
- Your country of birth
- Your language
- Your religion
- What your parents and family taught you when you were growing up
- How you were taught things at school

- The media you consume (TV, newspapers, films)

The first box you are programmed into is that of nationality. If you are told you are American or French or British, that comes with a whole load of things you have to "be" and ideas you have to buy into. You have constitutions, laws, ways of behaving, and all of these things make you distinctly nationalised. The truth is you are a homo sapien and you live on a planet called Earth; everything else is a man-made construct created for control and power. That's it! First program destroyed.

Where you were born is the next level of programming. Were you born in Texas, California, Yorkshire, Bordeaux, Andalucía, Sicily? When you look at your identity, you will find all sorts of belief systems and programs related to just the place you were born. More boxes, more programs, more baggage. Again you can treat this as you did nationality; it's completely meaningless drivel. If you are now saying "No, I am proud of being a Yorkshire man. I believe in that" well fine, believe in that and accept the programming that goes with that. If that program makes you happy and you are happy to make that part of your authentic self, then go ahead. But just be aware of what it is.

Your language also programs you. Having lived in many different countries over the years, I have learned that different languages have different ways of expressing things simply because of the language itself. Therefore, by just speaking a different language you will start to see the world in a different way. This is important because in some ways you are a prisoner to your own language unless you choose to learn another one. The best way to do that is to move to another country. This is an excellent way of realising what version of programming you have. Suddenly, you are in another region of the world with different programs, and this throws your existing thinking patters off balance.

Religion is another strong program instilled at birth. You shouldn't be afraid of religion. All religion comes from real life and is based on really sound advice. The bit you have to ignore is the big bird in the sky stuff. If you go back through all religions to the source some 10,000 years ago, there are texts and books that read like physics lessons. They knew 10,000 years ago about the cosmos, about sustainability, about ecosystems, about quantum physics – none of this stuff is new. The bit that is new is that over the last 2,500 years we realised that, if we control this information and create a beautiful story around it, we can get a lot of people to conform to a way of thinking. I once read an excellent book that put forward the following theory. Back when we started to get together in slightly larger groups, a new form of government was needed to manage the expanding villages and to control the growing societies. At the time we were quite a superstitious lot and thought that things like exploding volcanoes meant that the spirits were angry and so on. We had a spirit for everything and everyone believed something different. "God" was an excellent way of unifying all of this and getting rid of the proverbial chicken bones that the soothsayers threw around. God was powerful and people should fear him. God also had rules that meant some sort of order was created. The nub of this story is that God was created to introduce the first universal laws of society – and we haven't let go of them since. That's partly because the rules are good advice and partly because we are still at heart quite a superstitious lot. (Do you walk under a ladder?) The reality is that there is good advice everywhere and religion is not the only source of it. Faith and belief in the wider cosmos and the ethereal nature of our surroundings can all be done without an all-powerful God. Again, I am not telling you to abandon your faith if you have one; I would never do that. But I am asking you to acknowledge it for what it is and either accept all of it, part of it, or just bits of it, depending on what you think is useful. It is not an all-or-nothing proposition. Remember, faith is a great comfort to many people and offers advice and logical explanations for things that happen in daily life. The question is: are you blindly accepting faith or just accepting the bits that are useful?

If religion wasn't enough, then some of the rubbish your parents pumped into you is even worse. Well, let's be clear, parents only want the best for their children. When we lived in caves the knowledge that was passed on from one generation to another was fairly consistent. Nowadays, however, the question of what your parents pass down has to be questioned simply because the world changes so fast it's almost impossible to give good advice. What worked for your mother and father may not work for you in the world you are now growing up in. Take this book for example, this book is a father passing on to his son those things he thinks are important. It doesn't mean I am right or that you need to accept my programming; you have to make the decisions yourself based on what resonates with you. For example, if your parents told you that "the early bird gets the worm", and as a result you drive yourself to get up at 5 am every morning (despite the fact that you know you are a night person and you feel awful getting up early) then this is an example of programming you should reject. There are thousands of other examples and you should keep a journal handy and write them down as they come to you. They are all examples of things that have been drummed into you from birth that govern how you behave today. You need to flag them, analyse them and decide whether you are going to accept them as part of your programming.

School is another one. In the West we have a tradition of what is called Newtonian thinking. (Yes, named after the guy who discovered gravity.) It is what is called "reductionist thinking". We think that by analysing a problem – breaking it down into its smallest parts and understanding it – we can master it. In the world of work we have analysts, six sigma experts, process experts, all these people that will come and analyse a problem to death and tell you the answer. They will tell you what is true or not. It might surprise you to hear that in other parts of the world people are taught the exact opposite: that there is not one truth but many truths, and that you cannot break down a problem and discover the truth – sometimes you have to assume a truth and carry on with life, while testing real life against your assumptions and changing your view of what is true as you gain more information. This has a name too. It's called "Singerian fundamentalism", and it is a totally different way of thinking. You learn about this sort of stuff if you ever decide to do an MPhil or a PhD at university, but personally I think it should be taught at kindergarten. So you are now starting to see how far down the rabbit hole this programming business goes.

Finally, in order that I don't write an entire book on this, we come to media. Let's just be clear here: anything you read, watch or listen to contains programming. Just remember that. Always ask yourself: Why do they think that? Why are they telling me that? What do they want me to think?

Just ask yourself why the Chinese guys in Hollywood movies are no longer the bad guys? Well, China owns a large part of Hollywood now, and they don't want to be seen as the bad guys anymore on the world stage. So the next movie you see where a nation is being portrayed as "the bad guys", just remember, you are being programmed through your entertainment system.

17

Authenticity

Authenticity is one of the hardest things to achieve. As young men, we spend many years searching for it. We ask ourselves certain questions. Who am I really? What sort of person am I? Should I dress like this or like that? Should I like this or that?

The problem you have is that you are bombarded daily by messages from the corporate world and social media telling you to "be this" or "be that". It has got to the stage now that if you decide to revolt against all of that programming, they even have messages and guidance on what you can become instead. The reality is that the modern world wants you to be in a box, to lift a self-identity from the predetermined pile and decide "that's who I am!" They do this for a reason. Because once you have decided which identity to adopt, they have a super line of clothing and accessories to sell you so that you can look the part and everyone can look at you and go, "Oh, he's one of those", and you can identify with other people who have chosen a similar identity.

Initially, if you do that, you will feel comfortable for a while, but that has nothing to do with your identity; it just has to do with suddenly being accepted into the fold by the system around you.

Becoming your authentic self takes most of your life. You simply do not have time in your life to let others tell you what you should be. These are all blind alleys and time wasters. We all travel down a blind alley from time to time, and if they serve any purpose at all, it is only to teach you that you are not that sort of person and that can you continue your journey in another direction.

Becoming authentic is actually a reasonably simple process – although quite a long one – but the principle holds throughout your life. It boils down to this question: Do I want to do this – that is, is it something I will enjoy doing or need to do for myself?

If you keep asking yourself this question as you go about your daily life, you will quickly see that you are doing a multitude of things that you don't want to do. You are working against your authentic self. So, in small steps, you need to start writing down the things you don't want to do and all the things you do want to do. We never get to do everything we want, but at least knowing what we want allows us to make decisions that will make us happier.

As you begin to do this process, you will start to find yourself telling people around you what you want and don't want. Then, either friends will disappear or new ones will be formed, all on the basis of shared values and needs. As you go through this process you will start to evolve as a person. This will take years, but as long as you are moving in the right direction you are starting to evolve into your authentic self. You will develop ideas and views on the world based on what you like and dislike, and you will start to share them with people. You will start to live your life in a certain way according to what you like doing and want to do. These are all forms of authenticity.

Some of the most authentic people around defy categorisation. Quite often they are simply labelled as "eccentric". That's the box where we put people when either we can't explain them or they simply don't conform to the stereotypes we want them to. There is nothing wrong with being eccentric and you certainly don't have to work at it. Being eccentric is just you living your authentic life and saying "To hell with the rest of you and your crazy ideas; I'm living my life the way I want to".

Being authentic is one of the highest forms of honesty a man can achieve. Authenticity is reliable, dependable and honest in nature. You are who you are, and people can see that you are living your life not according to some social media trend or capitalist marketing brochure, but according to the things you want to do, the values you have and the beliefs you hold. In a way it is simple. Just remember authenticity is a life-long journey which starts the moment you decide to become the person *you* want to be rather than what *others* want you to be.

By following the guidance in this book, you will be on your journey to becoming your authentic self. There is no greater feeling in this life than eventually feeling comfortable in your own skin. There is a deep sense of contentedness at doing so, and this feeling radiates to everyone around you. It is a sign that you have mastered much of the world around you and gained enough wisdom to be able to just **be yourself**.

18

Integrity

I see integrity as a very personal thing. It is something that comes from deep inside you and reflects your values. The simplest way I can describe this is through an example. If one day you are asked to do something that perhaps requires you to lie about something, but deep inside yourself you feel uncomfortable doing this because it feels wrong, then refusing to do it will allow you to maintain your integrity.

Integrity comes from the word integral which means "whole". The idea is that by remaining true to yourself you keep yourself whole.

So often in life we are asked to do things that make us uncomfortable, but for one reason or another we go along with it, and we end up doing things because we are asked or forced to do so. Each time you do this you lose a bit of yourself, and gradually over time you become "undone". There is no longer enough of the original "you" to remain integral. You have in effect lost your integrity. You are now a mess of conflicting values and ethics based on the compromised decisions you have allowed yourself to make over past years. I strongly believe that this is at the heart of many psychological issues that people suffer in today's society, and a lot of psychiatry is about putting you back in touch with yourself – the original self that you lost.

Although this is a hard one to implement – as it requires you to have enough self-awareness to be able to define who you are to start with – it is really important that you maintain your integrity. When you decide that something is important to you – and this may be something as simple as being kind to other people – then you need to protect that part of you going forward, as it is now part of your integrity. So when you come across a situation where you are being pushed into being cruel to someone, you should protect your integrity by refusing to do it. When people start to see that you behave according to your values and self-identity, they will start to recognise you as a man of integrity – someone who is trustworthy because he will not compromise himself.

There is another benefit to maintaining your integrity and that is the satisfaction you feel when you have not done something to compromise your integrity. This sounds great, but it is not always easy. I have talked people through some really tough life-decisions where they have sacrificed a lot to maintain their integrity; however, afterwards all of them have said that it was like having a weight lifted off them once they had done the right thing. The thing that had been putting so much pressure on them wasn't what they might lose; it was actually the pressure they were putting on their conscience by having to seriously consider doing something they didn't want to do. Once you have done this a few times, you recognise how powerful protecting your integrity is, and it gets easier to make those decisions. You also find you get a lot more respect from those around you when you act with integrity.

Being a good man requires a level of integrity. Again it is one of those things that requires you to know who you are in yourself, what you believe in and what you are prepared to do and not do. That is why I always recommend that as you progress through life you think about things that define you, write them down and make a conscious effort to live your life according to those principles. You will be a lot happier when you do.

19

Trust

This is so important it could be a book on its own. Trust is what our life on this planet is based on; without it we are all doomed. It should be one of your foundation blocks as a young man. It is one of your most precious resources, both to give and to receive. You will find life very difficult if people do not trust you, so you simply must do everything you can to gain and earn trust from people.

Trust is actually very easy to earn and in most cases it is simply about being truthful and doing what you promised to do. If you just do those two things you will earn people's trust and good things will flow from it. In all honesty, I find it hard to understand why this seems difficult for people, but it seems to be so for some reason.

So, in a nutshell, if you want to be regarded as a trustworthy man – and who wouldn't want that – you need to be honest and you need to do what you promised to do. In a way trust is like your credit rating; if you have five star credit it means that the banks will lend you money because they know you are very likely to pay them back when you have agreed to do so. Well, people operate like that too They will give you time, money and opportunities if they believe you have a five star trust rating. If you score low on your trust rating then you will never know what you are missing out on because none of those opportunities will ever be presented to you. The other thing about trust is that very few people actually sit you down and explain why they don't trust you; they simply pass you over and go with people they trust.

One day you may decide to get married. Marriage is totally based on trust on many levels. You have to trust each other to be faithful and to do whatever is necessary to support each other. These are your marriage vows; they are basically a promise of trust between two people.

Trust is a funny thing, and many people think that they can mend trust if they break it; I don't believe you can. It is not something you can put back to the way it was before it was broken. The trust you mend is never as strong as the trust you earn to start with. Once you break trust it is a very serious matter with huge repercussions. It is for this reason that I really do urge you to do whatever is necessary to avoid breaking trust with people. If you can do this, you will save yourself a lot of trouble in life and attract a great deal of opportunity and enjoyment as a result.

There's nothing much more to be said on the matter. Trust is so important that you simply cannot afford to be without it or to break it – and if you do, prepare for problems in your life. You have been warned.

20

Loyalty

This is one to be careful with as it is something that is abused on a daily basis by friends and employers. The number of times I have come across young men in jobs where they are miserable and being treated terribly by their employer but they don't feel they can leave their job because, as they say, "I'm loyal", and for some reason they believe they will be rewarded for this.

Let's be quite clear: **Loyalty is a two-way street.**

Loyalty is something that builds up over time and is made up of many little events where you and another party show your loyalty to each other. You both go out of your way to stand up for each other and help each other. This is not an easy thing to do as there are so many events in life that require you to sacrifice something in some way for the other party: either money, time, effort, confrontation, support, sacrifice. So loyalty is something that is earned, not something that is given.

If you find you are feeling loyal to someone or an organisation, then you should expect to see some form of loyalty back. Going back to the example of young men stuck in jobs they don't like, an employer giving you a pay check is not a form of loyalty or something that loyalty can be expected for. You give your time in return for a wage; loyalty is another thing altogether. Now if you need to take time off work, for example, and it is longer than the statutory amount and your employer says, "take all the time you need Your job will be here when you get back," then that is a form of loyalty. That is an offer of loyalty to you as an employee. If you take that offer, then you need to reciprocate that loyalty at a later date. This way you deepen the bond of loyalty between you and the employer. But be careful because a company is not a person. Just be sure who you are being loyal to, the person making the offer or the company. I have seen people being loyal to a company because of a decision made years ago by a manager who has since left. In this case, the young man was still loyal to a company that was no longer loyal to him; it was the with manager who had left years ago that the bond of loyalty belonged.

Loyalty once again is a bond of trust. You will see throughout this book that trust underpins almost all aspects of being a good man. Society itself becomes undone if we lose trust in each other. Loyalty is a deep form of long-term earned trust between individuals and groups.

You see a lot of movies where gangsters demand loyalty, and this is normally enforced with the threat of something nasty if you are disloyal. Well, that is not loyalty to my mind; that is a form of compliance through fear, and when the chips are down and it's your life or theirs, you will abandon that sort of loyalty in a nano second. This is why most criminal fraternities come undone in the end: they are based on false loyalty.

I hope you can start to see that loyalty is an honourable and noble thing between people, a long term endeavour which is tested over time and proven to be durable and trustworthy. This is why it is such an important thing for you to cultivate with friends and close associates. It will support and sustain you throughout your life.

21

Responsibility and accountability

These are generally words you will hear in the work place, but I think they are just as important in your everyday life. They are the two words that account for the biggest messes in our lives.

I love this little joke about it, as I think it sums up the problem very neatly.

> This is a little story about four people named Everybody, Somebody, Anybody, and Nobody. There was an important job to be done and Everybody was sure that Somebody would do it. Anybody could have done it, but Nobody did it. Somebody got angry about that because it was Everybody's job.
> Everybody thought that Anybody could do it, but Nobody realised that Everybody wouldn't do it.
> It ended up that Everybody blamed Somebody when Nobody did what Anybody could have done.

You will be surprised at how many times this scenario will play out in your life and all because people don't like taking responsibility for things and being held accountable for their actions.

In my mind the mark of a leader of men, a man of distinction, is someone who steps up when required and agrees to take on whatever needs to be done and makes it his responsibility to deliver whatever has been agreed to be delivered. Trust me, everyone loves that person – for the simple reason that they don't have to do it! But if you want to have a successful life and career, then taking responsibility for things and accepting the accountability that comes with it are defining characteristics of success and are highly valued attributes in society.

If you need an example of how much you appreciate this in your everyday life, think of a situation where you have had a problem – it might have been a problem with your mobile phone, or with customer service, or something that you are trying to get sorted. You are getting passed from one person to another and no one is helping, and you are starting to tear your hair out. Finally, you come across someone who says, "Look, I'm going to sort this out for you. It's not my job and I'm not sure how we are going to do it yet, but leave it with me. I'll get this sorted." When you hear this, you almost start crying as all your frustration and anger disappears and you want to hug the other person. That feeling of relief and gratitude is generated simply by someone taking responsibility and accountability for a problem or for an action that is required, and making it his or her purpose to deliver a solution.

You can be that person who makes people feel like that. It is always your choice what you decide when and what you decide to take responsibility for, and what level of accountability you are prepared to accept. But always remember, out of a group of many, there are only a few people who are prepared to take on the challenge, and it is the mark of a special person who does.

22

Selfishness

To some degree or another we are all selfish. We always look after number one (ourselves) first. It is the default setting biologically; after all, it is what allows us to survive.

The problem with selfishness is that it isn't a very good trait in a developed society. Cooperation and sacrifice actually work better in a society. An even bigger problem is that capitalism wants us all to be "individuals" and to have whatever we need – as in the famous quote from the film *Wallstreet*: "Greed is good."

I am not saying that you shouldn't be selfish – that is actually impossible to achieve. There will always be a level of self-serving going on, no matter how generous and kind hearted you are. No, what I am advocating however is *less*-selfishness.

This is an incredibly hard thing to achieve as it covers so many aspects of your life. Here are the elements of your life where you can be less selfish:

- Time
- Love
- Desires
- Money
- Career

- Help
- Support

You will be selfish in all these areas to varying degrees, and it is up to you to decide where to draw the line. What are you prepared to give and what are you not prepared to give? Some of you will be more generous than others, and often your decision will depend on the person or organisations you are dealing with. One thing is for certain, there are two types of people in this world: givers and takers. Takers are always on the lookout for givers as they regard them as ATMs that don't need a passcode. So if you are naturally a giver, you probably need to introduce a level of selfishness to your life in order not to be taken advantage of. If you are a taker, then this is not a source of pride and it certainly is not a trait a respectable young man should have, so you need to work on being less selfish.

You might wonder why this chapter is about being only less selfish. Well, I think the world is far too selfish for its own good. Mankind has almost destroyed the planet in an act of ultimate selfishness. So when you reach for the cheap clothing in a shop, you are potentially being selfish because you are effectively saying your desire for cheap clothes is worth more than the sweatshops and working conditions that made them. When you eat a large steak, you are effectively saying that your desires are greater than the needs of the planet or the animal you killed for it.

Selfishness can be attributed to all aspects of our lives. It is not always obvious how we are being selfish, but we are most of the time. So the lesson here is to work on identifying how you are being selfish and maybe moderating it.

Ask yourself:

- Is what I want harming anyone else around me?
- Is what I am doing potentially harming others or things that I cannot see?
- Is there anything I can do to avoid harming others?
- Is there anything I can do to be less selfish about the choice I want to make?
- Am I being taken advantage of by someone else's selfishness?
- Will I allow someone else to take from me in this way?

Ultimately, you have to make choices that you are comfortable with and which others are comfortable with too. So be aware and try to give of yourself whenever possible as we all benefit from giving.

23

Change

A Greek philosopher called Heraclitus once said "The only thing that is constant is change." Never a truer word has been uttered.

Your life will be dominated by change, so don't get too comfortable. Change is neither good nor bad; it is just part of living. You may sometimes feel that changes have made your life harder, but at other times change may make your life easier. The thing to remember is that life will continually move and change like this. You must enjoy it when times are easy and you must persevere when times are hard. I am a strong believer that, over your life time, things are generally better than worse.

Here's the key to understanding change: **Within 3 months of a change occurring, you will find your mind adapting to the new reality.**

What this means is that change only seems better or worse for a short period before we get used to our new situation. You will then find benefits in your new situation that you didn't have in your old situation, which then means that you stop holding on to the past and embrace the future.[7]

---

[7] It is important to note that I am talking about the trials and tribulations of everyday life. If you are kidnapped by terrorists and subjected to daily beatings and torture, then this rule probably will not apply!

If you are one of the few people who lives in the past and always holds on to the past, valuing what you've had rather than what you could have, you will suffer greatly in life. The trick is to let go of what was and become what is, or could be, and to do that you must accept things. Fighting for things you have lost is a pointless exercise; let them go. You will find all sorts of help and "change curves" online that talk about the stages of change – and to be fair we do go through these curves – but the sooner you accept the change and embrace the new reality, the quicker you go through the stages and the less debilitating the change is for you.

Accepting change is a hard thing to do, partly because you have invested so much effort in getting to where you were that you get angry because you can't hold on to it. You have to practise and learn to let go. This is one of the greatest skills you can learn for yourself, and it will result in you being a calmer and happier person. It may even allow you to live longer.

So look for the changes that are coming, prepare for them and embrace them when they come. Don't look back – you are not going backwards. Look forward with an open and accepting mind. Your leadership in times of change is a strength that others can hang on to. Being able to let go and embrace new situations is a sign of strength and wisdom – something that a man should have at his disposal.

24

Acceptance

We really are bad at acceptance. As we discussed in the chapter on change, we hold on to our views of the world a long time after the world has moved on and it makes us very unhappy. We need to practise acceptance in order to move on with our lives.

How often has something happened to you and for the next few weeks you have raged about it with your friends and anyone else who will listen to you? If you are anything like me, it's fairly often. Just think how much time, stress and anger you created and how useless it was in the end. It got you nowhere, the changes happened and your behaviour had no effect on the end result at all.

The key to acceptance is realising that you cannot change what has changed, and rather than getting yourself worked up about, ask yourself this simple question: what does this mean I have to do now, instead? This way you focus on the new behaviours required rather that getting upset about the changes to your old behaviours.

I can tell you this as a certainty as I have spent almost thirty years as a change management consultant. My job is to change organisations so that they perform better. In all that time I have not managed to find anyone who believed that the changes that were coming could not be resisted by them. I tell them that I have been involved in change projects for thirty years and I explain that the changes are going to happen, whether they like it or not. But it doesn't seem to matter what we are told because we are programmed to resist change. We simply don't believe what we are hearing, and as a result we tend to suffer throughout the process until the changes are completed.

So here is a secret. When someone tells you that change is necessary or that things have changed, instead of saying "Well, I'm not doing that!" ask "What are the changes, how will they affect me, and what can I do to succeed going forward?" By doing this you will have changed your mindset from one of resistance to one of acceptance, and from that moment on you will be working to integrate yourself into a new way of working or living.

Okay, there is a "but" here. Sometimes the changes that are being foisted on you are unjust or just plain bad. If this is the case – and you need to be sure it is – then by all means resist. But make sure you know what you are resisting. Often I have found myself getting upset about something, and then, after I have spent a few weeks reading up and around the subject, I have decided that actually it is a really good idea and have ended up supporting it. So sometimes becoming more informed about change leads you down an easier path of acceptance.

Sometimes acceptance is only possible with forgiveness.

As a man, not accepting things can mean you become quite loud and aggressive. You need to be aware that as a large, strong individual, getting angry and marching about the place is quite intimidating for people around you and really not the sort of behaviour people want to put up with on a frequent basis. So by teaching yourself to be more accepting, you will have an calmer outlook on life – a more considered outlook – and other people will looked up to you as an example of someone who has a more enlightened approach to life. This is the sort of behaviour we want to achieve as men. Resorting to caveman antics is all too easy to do; the more sophisticated approach is the one I have outlined in this chapter.

25

Fairness

Fairness is a great, but not an easy, skill to master. It requires an ability to see things from different points of view. It also requires a strong underpinning of morality – the ability to discern right from wrong at a basic level. I feel that today there is an over reliance on lawyers to deliver what we hope is justice. I strongly believe that most people are capable of delivering their own justice through an understanding of fairness. If you deal fairly with everyone you meet and have an expectation of fairness in the way you are dealt with, then you will, for the most part, avoid costly lawyers and advisors trying to find resolution to problems you have got yourself into.

There is a concept of fairness in law called "equity". It is an appeal to the judge for fairness where the law has effectively gone down a blind alley and is about to deliver an injustice. "Equity" requires us to take a step back and to apply some common sense. It requires us to ask, what would be a fair outcome in this matter? After we have decided what the best outcome for all parties could be, we then go back and try to work out how we got it wrong, and we pass a new law to avoid the same mistake happening again.

We need to apply the same principle of equity in our lives in order to be fair to people around us as well as to ourselves. I believe the key to finding fairness in a situation is to try hard not to come to a quick decision about things where injustice is present. What I have found over my fifty years is that you rarely, if ever, have all the facts at your disposal. On top of that, the people giving you information are also biased about what they think. When it all comes down to it, you need to give yourself enough time to dig into the real facts and not the opinions, and to map out the story as it happened. Once you have done all of this and you start to see the situation from multiple angles, it becomes easier to see where fairness lies in the situation.

Sometimes I park a problem for a few days and during this time various insights come to me when I think of the problem from different angles. Nine times out of ten, after those few days I come to a very different conclusion to the one I was holding to start with. In today's society, where everything happens so quickly, it is very easy to fall into the trap of making snap decisions. Please don't do this; it makes you look stupid and gets you involved in a lot of mess which most of the time you don't need to be involved in at all.

The ancient Greek philosopher Socrates had some very good advice on the subject of finding truth and fairness in situations. There is a story that has been passed down through the ages that goes something like this:

> One day a man came to Socrates to share with him some really juicy gossip about a situation he had found out about. Before the man could speak Socrates asked him a question: "Before you speak of this you

must pass the triple filter test. First, have you made absolutely sure what you are about to say is true?" The man replied, "Well, no, I just heard—" At this point Socrates cut him off and asked another question: "Is what you were about to tell me kind or good?" The man looked at Socrates and shook his head. Again Socrates asked another question: "Is the information you were going to tell me useful or necessary for me to have?" And again the man shook his head. Socrates then said, "So, you don't know whether what you are going to tell me is true or not, you know that it is unkind and you know that it is neither useful nor necessary for me to know. Why then do you think I would be in any way interested in what you have to say. It is better you say nothing."

In the same way that Socrates acted, so must you with most of the information you receive in this world:

- Is it true?
- Is it kind?
- Is it useful?
- Is in necessary?

If what you are being told doesn't pass the test, you should know that what you are hearing probably is not fair either. You are more likely to be fair in your dealing with the people around you if you apply these filters to yourself as well as to others.

If you are fair as a man, people will trust your judgement. This is really important as it draws people towards you. Everyone needs help in finding their way through life's challenges, and being a man who can always be relied upon to find a fair outcome or see through a problem fairly is a great skill to have. You will become the arbitrator of arguments and the finder of solutions for people. And that has to be a good reputation to have.

26

Self-control

We are all impulsive at heart. We reach for the chocolate when we want a sweet. We like to have the things we want if they are available. We are taught at an early age that success is about getting what we want. Let me tell you from experience, having everything you want can be a mixed blessing.

Self-control is the measure of a man who has mastered himself. I'm not sure that you can actually implement any of the aspects of this book without mastering self-control. It is one of those aspects of character that takes some people a lifetime to master and even then not always successfully. I am not advocating denial here – I don't think denying your needs and wants is healthy either, and that is why I advocate moderation in another chapter. No, self-control is about being conscious of the things you are feeling and thinking, and deciding consciously whether they are the correct things to be doing or wanting at this time and juncture in your life.

We have all felt the urge to punch someone on the nose for whatever thing they have done to us, and luckily most of us manage to control this urge or we would all be walking around battered and bruised. So we are all capable of a measure of self-control, and sometimes it is the threat of the consequences that leads us to question our own desires at that moment in time and to "pull the punch". All I am advocating is an increased awareness that self-control applies all the time in everyday situations.

So, for example, when someone asks you a question, you have a choice how you answer it, or whether you answer it at all. Most of us are trained to answer a question when it is asked. But this isn't a rule. You don't have to answer it at all. You can just ignore it if you choose. Sometimes we say things because we feel we ought to, but on reflection we realise we really shouldn't have said them, or could have said them better, or in a kinder or more balanced way. Remember Socrates' triple-filter test in the fairness chapter: taking a moment, pausing to consider what your action is going to be and whether it is the right action at that moment in time is a powerful act of self-control – a conscious decision to act, rather than a reflex. The more important the decision or action you have to take, the more time you should give yourself.

Self-control applies to words, responses to others, your buying behaviour and almost all aspects of life.

Here is an example of a form of self-control I put in place for myself when I was a young man to stop me buying things. Whenever I had the urge to buy something, I asked myself this question: do I need it or do I want it?

Nine times out of ten I didn't need it, I only wanted it, so I wouldn't buy it unless I decided I was treating myself. This was a way of introducing a level of conscious self-control. It was my two-filter system as opposed to Socrates' three-filter system. I believe we can all create these little questions for ourselves to bring awareness to our actions and allow us to exercise a level of self-control.

Watching a man consciously exercise self-control in a situation is a truly spectacular experience, especially when he is a powerful individual, capable of wielding that power in devastating ways. The best example I can give of this is when you *want* to lash out at someone either verbally or physically, but instead you control that urge, find calm and step back. This is the mark of a man in control of himself and his surroundings.

27

Moderation

Moderation is not the same as self-control, although it does often require a level of self-control in order to be moderate in your appetites.

Moderation is something you will not be encouraged to do. We live in a capitalist system where curbing your appetite for life is not conducive to growth in the economy. You will be encouraged to "maximise your potential", "extract maximum enjoyment", "be your best self", and so on. All of these messages are designed to encourage you to consume and set no limits on yourself.

You are talking to someone who spent thirty years of his life doing exactly this. If there was a job worth doing, I did it to the maximum. I ate, drank, partied and worked like a monster in that time. And eventually it almost killed me. When you are young your body can withstand enormous amounts of punishment, and you recover. But what you don't see is that slow and cumulative effect it is having on your body. Health is not how we are taught to perceive it. We think that as you get older things gradually start to go a little bit wrong, and you need a few pills for this and that, and then just before you die most things are going wrong, and that is generally when you get ill.

Well, I am sorry to break your bubble but health sort of works like the following: everything is fine, everything is fine, everything is broken.

Once you lose your health, you never really get it back like before. You just lose it.

So why am I talking to you about health in a chapter on moderation? Well, it turns out that moderation is one of the keys to a long and healthy life. If you moderate your stress levels, alcohol consumption, make healthy food choices, work in moderation, and so on, your body will have a chance to look after you.

Working for 24 hours a day, 7 days a week, 365 days a year is not moderation. Moderation is working 8–9 hours a day, 4.5 days a week. Moderation is getting 8 hours sleep a night rather than 4 – because you are a party animal. Drinking enough to have a good time but not enough to get a hangover the next day is moderation. Drinking once a week rather than every night is moderation. If you are a smoker, smoking one or two cigarettes a day rather than twenty to forty is moderation. Stopping eating before you explode and feel ill is moderation.

In the end, it is your choice whether you exercise a level of self-control over yourself and moderate your behaviour. All the information is out there if you need it, but you have to want to do it. Trust me, if you don't moderate your behaviour, at some time in the future, your body will do it for you, and you will find that you just simply won't be able to do all the things you want to do anymore.

The way I had to deal with this crisis in my life was to set up what I call a "standard day". This evolved, not through any conscious effort on my part, but simply by working to what my body was capable of letting me do. I found that I could only really function if I woke up at 7 am and had two hours to have breakfast and get to work. I found that I needed to have lunch and couldn't go all day without it like I used to. I found that gluten, dairy, meat and alcohol affected me badly, making me bloated, sluggish and asthmatic, so I had to go vegan. I realised that I needed nine hours of sleep at night. I had to eat a light supper before 7 pm. I realised that, if I was travelling to work each week, I had to work from home one week in every five, I realised that I couldn't handle stress very well anymore. All of these things were taught to me as a result of the health crisis I had, and it has all led to me having what I call a "standard day". My standard day is an exercise in moderation, and as a result of running my life like this, I now am able to live a happy and fulfilled life, to work and to enjoy myself. At the age of fifty-one I am now the same weight I was at twenty-one, and I am fitter than I have been in thirty years.

So I encourage you to introduce a level of moderation into your life. Find what works for you, listen to your body and adjust what you do so that you feel fresh, happy and healthy every day. What the grown-ups won't tell you – and what I call "the conspiracy of silence" – is that you have twenty-five good years where you are almost bulletproof physically. After that things start to go wrong. So you are clear until you are in your forties. If you implement a level of moderation in your life, I think you can probably get to your sixties without any problems at all. You probably get another twenty years of robust physical health without any problems, if you exercise moderation in your life.

If you don't believe me, just go around and ask any 50-year-olds you know whether they have any minor health problems. You will be surprised how many will tell you they have high blood pressure, high cholesterol, diabetes, asthma, erectile disfunction, are overweight and so on. It's just that we don't talk about these things in public. I wish we would, because we could stop our young men falling into the same trap.

Moderate your behaviour and live a long and healthy life.

28

Consistency

Consistency is not something that gets talked about much these days, but it is so important. Being consistent is part of being coherent as a person. How many of us have decided we are going to start running every day, or eating healthily every day – most of us, I would imagine. Well, how long did it last? Probably not very long.

You see we are by nature inconsistent. We find it hard to start something and maintain it. Well, I am here to tell you that great things are achieved through consistency. If you look at all the great athletes, they have trained consistently every day, for years and years, to achieve what they wanted. If you consider the great scientists or entrepreneurs, they have all achieved what they did by consistently working on what they needed to in order to achieve the results they got.

Being consistent is hard work. As a young man, you might be really focussed on achieving a certain goal. But you find that your friends are always asking you to come out with them, and you find that you are inconsistent in your efforts, so that your goal seems to get further and further away, until in the end you think, "What's the point, I'm never going to get there!" The truth is you failed because you didn't have the self-control, the discipline, the courage, the right friends to allow you to achieve your goal. It all conspired against you to stop you achieving what you needed or wanted to do.

When you hear about the stories of people going from rags to riches, there is a consistent theme throughout all their stories: they worked hard consistently for years, through all sorts of hardships, in order to achieve what they did. So I am not saying this is an easy trait or skill to develop in yourself; you need to be a fairly well-developed character in order to be consistent.

One of the nice things about consistency it that is generates trust in other people. If you can demonstrate consistency, then you are not regarded as someone who will change his mind or be whimsical. People will then entrust you with important tasks and invest in you because you are able to demonstrate on a daily basis a commitment to going about your life in a consistent and coherent fashion.

So try it. Pick some aspect of your life you wish to change, or something you want to achieve, and see if you can be consistent in your activity towards that goal either until it is achieved or for the rest of your life. You can take great pride in yourself if you do achieve consistency because, as I have already pointed out, you will have learned a great deal about other chapters in this book on the way to being consistent.

Consistency is a great trait in men. It shows discipline and focus, and is a source of trust for people. It means you are reliable and shows a level of maturity in your behaviour which implies a great deal of self-knowledge. It is a great skill to have and be able to demonstrate. You find that the bullshit artists of this world are very often completely inconsistent in the things they say and do – and there are, unfortunately, an awful lot of them about. So it is up to you to be better than that and show the world how consistent you can be when going about your daily life.

29

The internet of things

Unlike many of you, I was around before the Internet existed, so when it arrived, I can tell you it was one of the most exciting things to have happened in my life. When it first started, there were no shops and no online shopping. There was email, a rudimentary browser and a lot of people chatting on internet relay chat (IRC) and sharing files. It was a very exciting time for us. We could see how all of this sharing of knowledge and being able to talk to people on the other side of the world in real time was going to allow mankind to leap forward.

Less than twenty years later and the Internet is a TV and shopping centre for most people, a tool for governments to carry out misinformation wars, and a tool for politicians to use to confuse people. It enables all the kinds of lies and criminal activity we could ever dream of. And, worst of all, it all fits in your pocket and we all spend hours of our day consuming content from it.

In fact, it has not turned out to be how it was envisioned at all in the beginning. That of course doesn't mean that you can't *make* the Internet do what you want it to. You can choose news syndication apps, you can save bookmarks of reliable sources of news, you can even engage with some of the most renowned universities and organisations in the world. All you need to do is ignore all the rubbish. The Internet is one of the most remarkable tools available to us, and it is up to us to decide how it should be used. It is not for companies like Amazon or Apple to decide that for us. Companies have got very clever in producing all sorts of apps and services that they give away for free so that they can sell things to us and use our information.

Let's be clear, if you buy a computer or a smart phone, then you should be in control of what it does and how it is used. But so often we are not aware of how that simple choice is eroded through the choices that are presented to us.

So my advice to you is use the Internet and all its apps as a tool. Use it to learn stuff, use it to exchange information, on occasion use it to entertain yourself. But do not become a slave to it. And certainly don't let it control you.

Here are some things that can help you develop a healthy behaviour towards your technology:

- Write down what you are going to use the Internet for and stick to your rules.
- Designate a time limit for how long you will be online each day.
- Switch your phone off during certain times of the day and night.
- Leave your phone at home when you go out sometimes just to break the habit.
- Use your phone as a phone and call people rather than texting all the time.
- Buy a little camera – it will take better pictures and means you can buy a cheaper phone.

- Buy a kindle if you read a lot – or better still pick up a paperback as it doesn't need batteries.
- Don't buy anything you can't afford to lose.
- Don't commit your whole life to a phone – for example, if you are going to bank online make sure you have a laptop at home.
- Try if possible not to use social media – I promise you it is almost a total waste of time.
- Don't put all your information in the cloud – one day it will simply disappear.
- If it's free to use, you will be paying for it somehow.

Take it from me, I was around when the first portable computer was invented, I have been at the cutting edge of technology since I was eight years old. I love technology, so I am not telling you this because I am some old fart who hates all things tech. I have technojoy, but I also know how much time it wastes and how it can be used for less than honest reasons. So protect yourself, use VPNs, use encrypted email, encrypt your data, keep hard copies of important things, maintain local SSD storage backups and use very big passwords. Stay safe and enjoy yourself. (Sounds rather like the advice fathers give to their sons when they go out on a date!)

Nowadays, so many men are obsessed about their online image and keeping in touch with thousands of followers. When you look around on a bus or a train, everyone has their head in a phone or a laptop. No one speaks to each other. We can learn more about ourselves and others and the world around us by simply putting the device away and talking to the person in front of us. Some of the most enlightening conversations I have had in my life have come from talking to complete strangers in situations like the ones I describe. So, as a man, you need to take an interest in the world around you, and that does not necessarily have anything to do with your phone or the Internet.

30

The media

At one time in our history the media and journalists were regarded with some respect, but over the years this has been eroded. I blame the 24-hour news cycle for this, the poor men and women in this industry are under so much pressure to catch news as it happens and provide all day viewing that none of them have time to do their job anymore – which, by the way, is to investigate and report on news that we, as a viewer, should know about.

On top of this the media has always been a tool of governments and has been used extensively as a propaganda tool. It is not by accident that we have certain values and beliefs in our countries; our state media is there to sell and reinforce a certain set of values and beliefs that the government wants in its population.

I learned just how dishonest the media was when, as a young man, I spent the day in Trafalgar Square with families having barbecues and playing children's games as part of a "reclaim the streets" protest. I wasn't there for any other reason than that I happened to be walking by and thought this looked like a fun place to be on a sunny day. When I got home that night, the Nine O'clock News reported that there had been running street battles with police in the square that morning. It showed petrol bombs being thrown and baton charges by police. It reported that by

9.30 am the square had been cleared and normal traffic had resumed with no further incident that day. I couldn't believe what I was seeing, and when I looked closer I recognised that the footage they were using was from the Brixton riots a few years earlier. So in a nutshell, my national TV station had created a complete work of fiction and lied to 60 million people. It was on that day that I switched the TV off and threw it on the skip. I haven't watched TV for over thirty years now.

So when Donald Trump coined the phrase "Fake News" that is what he was talking about. What's more, news and media is now streamed to you through multiple channels and devices. You probably wouldn't think that Hollywood is a way of selling you ideas, but it's true. Just look at how baddies are dressed in black and goodies are in white in the old Westerns. Look at how the benefits of technology are sold to you through sci-fi movies and how "bad" Chinese people are running drugs cartels in the USA. (It used to be the Italians, then the Russian, then the Albanians – it changes according to who the government wants you to think are bad.)

So I have this really simple piece of advice for you. If you want to be happy and not stressed and fearful for the rest of your life, turn off the radio and the TV and stop watching news. When you are shown things, be aware that there is almost always bias, and sometimes even deliberate misdirection going on. Question everything; trust nothing. You will find that if a thing is important enough for you to know, the chances are you will find out about it through word of mouth or some reputable journalist or writer on the Internet a few weeks later after they have done some research.

    Media in this day and age is a form of social conditioning and programming (see Chapter 16 on programming). If you want to have a stress-free life and enjoy living in a modern society as a young man, you could do a lot worse than turn off the TV and radio. There are plenty of reputable sources of considered news available out there, so if you want to find out about something, don't just accept the rubbish that is channelled to you 24/7 – go in search of a reputable source of knowledge. If you want to be respected as a man who has a balanced and fair view of the world and who is trustworthy, then you need to be careful what you believe and where you get your information.

31

Government

You probably don't think much about government – or at least the role of government – even though you are bombarded by politicians all day long. The truth is that historically we used to have rulers – kings and queens or dictators who rolled over us. As the world's population grew "Statecraft" – which is what rulers practised to keep control of the masses – was getting harder to do. Simply killing people you didn't like was proving to be unpopular. So we came up with a concept called democracy, where people had the choice of who was going to represent them. This was a much better idea as at least we seemed to have some control over the people in power, and there were laws and rules around what people could or could not do. It has proven to be an excellent way of keeping most people happy most of the time in a reasonably fair way.

    Now, let's not kid ourselves, "statecraft" is alive and well. We still kill off people we don't like, and we censor people who are proving to be a pain. Our governments retain the ability to enlist their citizens into the army at a moment's notice if necessary, and if they think the threat is big enough, send them off to be killed. Don't kid yourselves, governments can take your property and everything you own, just like that.

It is really important for you to realise that you live the illusion of freedom. You are given this freedom because it is available to you at this moment in history. If anything, history has taught us that all of this can change in a New York minute. So it is really important that you live your life understanding that it is a privilege of your time in history and government that you live freely, are able to express your views and are able to do more or less what you want with your life. But it can all be taken away tomorrow.

I used to drink in my local pub in London with a guy from the US embassy. He was in charge of the fifty-year strategy for Africa. His job was to plan what was going to happen to Africa in the next fifty years and what the USA was going to do in Africa for the next fifty years. Think about this for a moment; governments plan things *fifty years ahead*. So when you see the news about an Arab spring, for example, and the news is telling you that, because of Facebook and social media and all these unhappy Arabs, they have chosen to overthrow their governments, you need to put this in historical perspective. What have people been doing for the last fifty years? And what does it look like they want in the next fifty? Social media had nothing to do with the Arab spring. If you want to know what governments are doing, you need to look back at least fifty years.

As normal people, thinking and planning over fifty years just isn't something we do. Our time-frames are much shorter. The longest we plan ahead is probably our annual holiday. Most of the time it's what we are going to do on the weekend. So you see our brains aren't even capable of joining the dots over 100 years of history to work out what our governments are up to. The lesson here is don't ever think that your government is incompetent; they are planning for the long term and implementing strategy over the long term. The sleight of hand they use is also another form of statecraft. As the ancient Romans would say, *Panem et Circenses* (Bread and Circuses) – they give you food and entertainment to keep you from seeing what is really happening and take your mind off things.

Why am I telling you all this depressing stuff? Well, it's because so many people today think that they have some inalienable right to freedom and that they can say and do anything. You can't; you are being allowed to do that. There is a big difference. If you ever want to know what it is like to take on the power of the state, then try to do something serious and you will find out how little power and freedom you have.

My message here is be informed and be respectful of the freedoms you have. Treat them responsibly and always be aware that they are a privilege not a right. I know this will really grate with some of the liberals out there but, let's face it, they are the first to get rounded up and shot when a government clamps down for some reason, so historically speaking they are the first to find out that they were not quite as free as they thought!

This is an important lesson for you to learn as it will introduce to you a level of cautiousness and approach that will allow you to go about influencing those that need influencing safely as well as keeping yourself safe too.

32

Timing

"Timing is everything." I am sure you have heard this phrase many times. Timing is not the same as time, we are not talking about calendars, hours and minutes, years and months. We are talking about the way the world works.

In a nutshell, what we are talking about is this: **You won't be able to get something done if the timing is not right.**

There are gurus all over the Internet that will tell you that hard work, getting up a 4 am and running 20 km, using time management systems, working efficiently and hard and so on will mean you always get what you are after.

Sorry, but that is absolute rubbish. I was one of those guys the gurus talk about. For me it was relatively easy, so I didn't really have to work very hard to be efficient. But I did learn one or two things along the way in my fifty years, and one of the main lessons was this: if the timing isn't right, it doesn't matter how hard you push, it won't happen.

So here are a few reasons why what I am saying is true. Generally speaking, what you are trying to achieve in life will almost always be dependent on others. Other people have different motivations and are also living in a larger connected economic system. Some aspects of the system can be overcome, some motivations of others can be overcome, but generally speaking if you are working your socks off and not making any progress, it is because your timing is off.[8]

In 2008 there was a worldwide financial crash. I thought that this would represent a great opportunity to grow my business. I invested thousands in marketing and sales activity. Probably ten times more than usual. It yielded nothing! Why? Because I hadn't realised that my timing was wrong. People were not ready. They were all panicking and trying to work out what to do. I had to close my business and retire for three years before the phone started to ring again. 2012 was the right time! But by that time I didn't have the same business anymore.

You have to pay attention. Sometimes you just need to work hard to earn a living and can't expect anymore. Sometimes you don't even have to work hard to earn a living. What most of us should do is work hard when times are easy, and relax and enjoy ourselves when times are hard. If you are ambitious, then when things feel easy this is your time to grow and work extra hard. When things are tough, then don't spend any more energy than what is necessary to get by. You will have to go through a few recessions and economic crises before you learn this lesson and are able to calibrate what is a hard period and what is an easy period. **Life is a balancing act and it really helps if you can get the timing right.**

There are things you can do to "game" the system. So if the time is not right for your skill or business, then look around for the people that are

---

[8] You may also be working on the wrong things, but let's assume you are working on the right things.

succeeding and, if you can, move into that space. What is poor timing for you might not be for others. Having this awareness will allow you to navigate the world more successfully.

Another form of timing I see is with employees. So many people hang on to jobs that most people can see are going to be made redundant. If the business you are in is not doing well financially, then that is the right time to get your CV out and look for another job. If you wait to be made redundant, that is the wrong time to look for a job. When you have a job, you are always both more employable and in a better negotiating position. You don't want to be in a situation where you are unemployed looking for a job, with mounting bills and dwindling savings, where you have to take the first job you are offered. You see, although timing is subtle, it can have profound effects on your life. So don't be scared of making big decisions if you think the time is right. On the other hand, if the whole economy is suffering and unemployment is at record levels, you might want to look at how you make yourself indispensable to your current employer and look at how you reduce your bills and save money.

My message to you is be aware. Be aware of what is going on, and how hard it is for you to earn a living. Be aware that the world moves in cycles and that there are good times and hard times. Be aware that not everyone has the same cycles, so there are always opportunities if you are quick and flexible.

33

Forgiveness

Who would have ever thought forgiveness could be so hard. We see families of murdered children forgive the killers every day and wonder how they can do that. How could you possibly forgive someone who killed your loved one?

Well it took me fifty years to learn what forgiveness is, how it works, and how to do it. I really wished someone had explained it to me properly when I was young. Everyone used to say, "You should forgive so and so." That was a bit like saying, "You should visit Timbuktu." The point I am trying to make is that if you have never heard of Timbuktu, you don't know if it's a physical place or an idea. You have no idea *how* to visit it, or what to do to get there. In fact, the advice is completely useless to you!

The Buddha (allegedly)[9] had something to say that has always resonated with me:

> Holding on to anger is like grasping a hot coal with the intent of throwing it at someone else: you are the only one who gets burned.

---

[9] I don't know whether the Buddha actually said this or something similar. It sounds sort of authentic, but that doesn't matter, it is ascribed to him and it is a really good piece of advice.

This all makes sense to me, but the bit I could never get my head around was *how* to forgive someone. How can you do it and somehow make it feel okay?

Well, the thing I learned is this: forgiveness is a choice that you give your subconscious and conscious mind. In any decision where forgiveness is necessary, there are two roads you can go down. The first road is one of anger, accusation, argument, pain and stress. The other road is one without all of those things. Why wouldn't you want to choose the road without the pain and stress? So you decide consciously to forgive the person even if you are still angry with them. Even at this stage your brain is furious and unwilling to let go. But you have decided, so you say to yourself: "I am not going to go down the endless road of pain and anguish. I am going to forgive the person and I am going to live with that decision."

Well, the moment you consciously decide this, something remarkable starts to happen over the coming weeks, months and years. Your brain actually starts to forgive the person. What happens is this: every so often your brain throws an idea at you that you hadn't thought about, and when you think about it you realise that it wasn't all the other person's fault. Bit by bit your view of the other person softens as you become more aware of your role in the situation, the roles of others and how the other person might have felt at times. All of these things start to build a picture. More often than not, you find that you feel compassion for the other person's point of view, and you eventually realise you have forgiven that person. **Forgiveness comes with greater awareness**.

On occasions, I have gone back fifteen years later and apologised to people about things they had completely forgotten about, because I realised I needed forgiveness rather than them!

Forgiveness is a very powerful intellectual exercise. It will make you much calmer and happier with the world. It requires you to have acceptance. It requires integrity, authenticity, courage, respect, compassion and a desire to be more than yourself. It is not by accident that the Christian faith hinges almost totally on forgiveness. You don't have to be religious, but you do need to learn one of the most important skills we have in our arsenal.

I have friends who haven't talked to their families for years because they cannot bring themselves to forgive. The trauma these people have when their parents die without ever having resolved their differences lives with the survivors for the rest of their lives. They then have to try to forgive themselves for their actions.

Don't hold a grudge, don't hold on to the hot coal, don't harm yourself, let go, forgive, move on and enjoy the life that is yours to enjoy.

Old chapters

I initially wrote three chapters on wokeness, sexuality and race. In the end, I included some of the text from these additional chapters in Chapters 5 and 7. However, I've decided to include the full chapters in their original version here because they resonated with a number of people I sent them to for review. Therefore, it's worth telling you a little about the chapters and why they are still in the book.

When I wrote this book, I was angry at the whole wokery nonsense, and this was brought on by the transsexual groups of people wanting to be called "they" and demanding things from society that I thought they really had no right to expect. I was severely miffed at the whole Black Lives Matter fiasco, which suddenly seemed to turn all of us white folks into racists overnight. I was reading a book by Ben Elton at the time called *Identity Crisis* and got so annoyed by the subject I felt I wanted to do something.

Over a period of time, I had a number of conversations with some young people and I realised they were all being affected by these minority voices and were getting confused. As a friend said to me: "This is just a handful of people who are using the Internet like a megaphone."

When I first wrote the chapters I felt I had dealt with the subjects fairly and robustly, and yet at the back of my mind something didn't feel right about it. So I rewrote them and then rewrote them again. In the end I came to realise that part of the problem was that I was actually now conditioned, through years of political correctness and wokery, to not really want to say how I felt about things. Also, I didn't want people to misread my intentions or views.

Then on further reflection, I thought, I can't put up with the amount of abuse the woke community are going to heap on me when I publish this.

In the end I think I did a better job with subject in Chapter 5 (Tolerance) and in Chapter 7 (Having an opinion), but I also lost something in the process which was my authentic voice – and this is the sorcery of wokery at work.

So I am leaving the original unedited chapters in the back of the book by way of being honest to myself. My intention is not to upset people and harm them, but I do feel I have right to express myself honestly. Plus I think there is a raw form of honesty in these chapters and that there are points made in these chapters that didn't make it into the rewrite.

I hope this makes sense.

"Wokeness" or "wokery"

Let's be quite clear, you really need to be some kind of idiot to even entertain the idea of wokeness. For a start, it isn't even a word. You might well awaken, be woken up, but you most certainly cannot *be* woke. This idea of wokeness – being sensitive to everything and not upsetting anyone – is in my view one of the worst kinds of insidious nonsense ever to be paraded around the global youth.

If you find that you are over sensitive and care so much about what others might think and that you are constantly considering your choice of words and language and worrying about whether you can say something or not, then you are in a prison of your own making. Let's be quite clear here, when you communicate with anyone, you generally do the best you can. Most people do not intend to upset or offend other people as this normally defeats the object of talking to another person. If by communicating generally and in good faith with others you find the other person is getting mortally offended by the words you use, then that is a problem *they have*, not you. They are the ones who are being disingenuous towards you. Communicating well is a very hard thing to do, and if you need to keep up with the continuously changing language of the day in order to be politically correct, you won't be communicating very much at all, I can tell you.

So here is a piece of advice: just talk, talk kindly and respectfully to people, and if they get upset, then just say, "I'm sorry you feel that way," and leave them alone.[10] People that are that easily offended will either seek out others who share their beliefs or become so lonely they won't care anymore about being offended and just be glad someone is talking to them at all.

You are not required to be woke. It is up to you whether you decide to use certain language or agree with certain points of view. You are entitled to have your own point of view, just as much as the population of snowflakes that perpetuate their nonsense. Just remember that 90 per cent of the globe have no idea what a snowflake is or what a woke person is, so you are in good company.

In another ten years, most of the "mortally offended" woke people will have given up and moved on to some other drivel that they can bore people with. You just need to get on with your life and not worry about offending people. People get offended all the time in life and part of your skills as a young man is dealing with being offended and moving on.

---

[10] Alternatively you can invoke the great Stephen Fry:
"It's now very common to hear people say, 'I'm rather offended by that.' As if that gives them certain rights. It's actually nothing more ... than a whine. 'I find that offensive.' It has no meaning; it has no purpose; it has no reason to be respected as a phrase. 'I am offended by that.' Well, so fucking what." From "I saw hate in a graveyard", Stephen Fry in *The Guardian*, 5 June 2005.

Sexuality

This subject has become the source of unbelievable confusion in today's world. We have a veritable alphabet soup of three letter acronyms to define our sexuality. You will have come across LGBTQ and more letters that I cannot remember. We are being taught that it is acceptable to be transsexual, bisexual, and whatever other descriptions exist out there.

If you are feeling confused, then welcome to the club. This subject can be incredibly complex, and if you are in a position of authority or within a school or institution, you are probably receiving training on how to be particularly sensitive in the language you use and how you approach these matters. One of the reasons I have included a chapter on wokeness is because I think this subject falls neatly into the category.

Well, let me try to make this easy for you. The gay community is estimated to be in the region of only 3.7 per cent of the global population. This is a very small minority group who have achieved an enormous amount in terms of gaining recognition and acceptance. But just to be clear, 3.7 per cent of the population does not mean that the rest of us need to change our behaviours and language or our self-identity. It simply means that a small number of people can now live their life in peace, free from persecution, with equal rights to self-expression, or at least should expect to be allowed to do so.

We are all free to become what we want in this world. This is a really important message: *Everybody* has a right to be the person they want to be.

What everyone does not have a right to do is change the world around them because of their choices. *You* have the right to be who you want to be too.

So this boils down to a simple premise: as long as you respect someone's right to be who they want to be, no matter how absurd it might seem to you, you can honestly expect the same right in return (you too have a right to appear absurd to others as well). You do not need to learn new ways of talking, you do not need to learn new words, and you do not need to be trained on how to act in this new world.

Fundamentally, we are all humans; there are men and women and children at the heart of this world. Everyone has a name, and we have a name so that we can address people with it. I have beautiful, fun and wonderful friends from the LGBTQ community, and they are wonderful because they are genuinely wonderful people; their sexuality is of no more concern to me than the sexual preferences of straight people. In fact, there is a wider question here: Why is what people do in the privacy of their own homes any business of outside observers anyway? If you find people kind, fun and supportive, then you should have no problem being friends with them.

Some of you will now be asking the question: But what if I am a gay man? Can't I be a man as well?

At the risk of opening up a debate, this book is written by a "straight" man for "straight young men" and as a result it is biased towards what my view of that role model should look like in the context of "straight males". I am not from the LGBTQ community, so I cannot give specific guidance to members of that community. All I can say is that I see no reason at all why anyone should not be able to identify with the principles outlined in this book. The book is not written in order to navigate the complexity of gender politics. Rather, it is written in a straightforward manner where gender is simply defined as male and female with clear role models for each. This is not a book written to be politically correct; it is written simply to give guidance to young men on how to better live their lives.

So to finish up, my young men: A man does not need to engage in hate speech, hatred or aggression towards fellow humans, and should never do so under *any* circumstances. In all the advice I give you throughout this book, you should apply it to all men and women of any colour, creed or persuasion. If you cannot do this, then you will never in my view earn the title of a proper man.

Race

Having talked about sexuality, I also need to address the other elephant in the room: race. I think I can deal with this one fairly quickly and simplistically as well.

If you hold any opinion other than "we are all equal", then I am afraid you are racist, my friend – and this *may* not be entirely your fault. In all probability, you will have been indoctrinated into this viewpoint from the moment you were born.

Having lived in eleven countries and visited over forty, I can honestly tell you this:

- Rule number 1: **Skin colour and ethnicity mean nothing**. Some of the most wonderful people I have ever met come from cultures completely different from my own. No matter the colour of your skin, you are human, you love your children and your family, you care for others, you like to celebrate, and you get old and die like everyone else.
- Rule number 2: **If you are a racist, then you simply cannot call yourself a real man**. You are instead a real racist – and trust me, that is not a nice thing to be.

So if you find yourself in the unenviable position of thinking that for some reason where you come from and what your skin colour is gives you some inalienable right over others, then you will need to do some hard work, probably for the rest of your life!

Take the time to get to know people in an honest and genuine way. You will find more similarities than you could ever imagine. Travel the world and meet people in their own countries, share in their hospitality and enjoy the experience of being part of a global community. You will become a better person for it.

A real man makes it his business to know other cultures and to experience as much of the world as he is able to do. Even if he has not had the opportunity to travel and interact with other cultures, he still offers hospitality and kindness to strangers he meets, irrespective of their colour or origin.

Gentlemen, this is *really* important: If you are a racist, you are not a man – you are less than a man. So start working on any prejudices you have – they have no role in your life or that of your children. And just to be clear, if you pass on racism to your children because you didn't do the hard work necessary on yourself, then you are not welcome in the brethren of men. Think about that carefully. There is no room anywhere on this planet for racism of any kind, in any form.

Printed in Great Britain
by Amazon